Your GRIT Gauge™ Access Code: qjnGLyyL
Enter at www.gritgauge.com

Also by Paul G. Stoltz

*Adversity Quotient: Turning Obstacles
into Opportunities*

*Adversity Quotient @ Work: Finding Your
Hidden Capacity for Getting Things Done*

*The Adversity Advantage: Turning Everyday
Struggles into Everyday Greatness*

*Put Your Mindset to Work: The One Asset
You Really Need to Win and Keep the Job You Love*

#1 NEW YORK TIMES BEST-SELLING AUTHOR
PAUL G. STOLTZ, Ph.D.

GRIT™

The New Science of What it Takes to
Persevere · Flourish · Succeed

CLIMB
STRONG
PRESS

Published by ClimbStrong Press, Inc.
www.climbstrongpress.com
info@climbstrongpress.com

ISBN: 978-0-9906580-0-9
First Edition

Printed in the United States of America

Author photo by Forrest L. Doud

DEDICATION

This book is dedicated to my father, Gary A. Stoltz,
whose simple mantra "You can do anything you
set your mind to" was the single greatest gift any son
could hope to receive. Papa, I will miss you terribly.

CONDENSED CONTENTS

FULL CONTENTS

INTRODUCTION—THE NITTY-GRITTY

YOUR GRIT GPS—MAPPING THE JOURNEY

SECTION TWO—ADVANCED

"I like things that make you grit your teeth.
I like tucking my chin in and sort of leading into the storm.
I like that feeling. I like it a lot."
— DANIEL DAY-LEWIS, WINNER OF
THREE ACADEMY AWARDS FOR BEST ACTOR

INTRODUCTION

The Nitty-Gritty

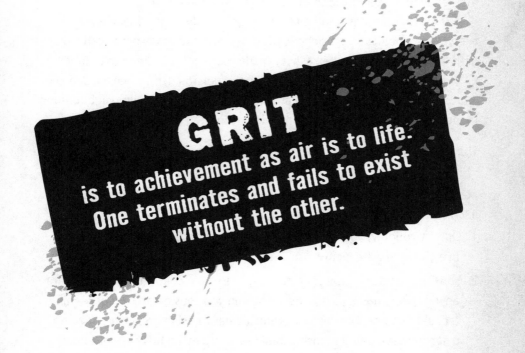

GRIT is to achievement as air is to life. One terminates and fails to exist without the other.

GRIT : Your capacity to dig deep, to do whatever it takes—especially struggle, sacrifice, even suffer—to achieve your most worthy goals.

It is nearly impossible to overstate or overestimate GRIT's power, reach, and influence. Ever had that eye-opening experience when you leave home for a period of time, only to notice things anew when you return? Where it's almost like being a tourist in your own town, or even your own home? Or when that long-awaited summer break between grades made you see your school differently the moment you walked through those doors again come fall?

For a brief moment, you had that invigoratingly bright, fresh lens on everything around you. Somehow, whatever you saw and experienced "out there," or simply the act of being away, made you see things differently "right here."

Now, let's try that with GRIT. Try looking through *that* lens. Given the definition above, turn on your GRIT radar. Scan for GRIT in your own family, neighborhood, friends, job, and community. You may be astonished by what you discover.

Take the GRIT Challenge

The GRIT Challenge is a simple game you can play to quickly and powerfully put GRIT into context. It involves four simple steps. Here's how it works:

1. Draw a (roughly) 50-mile radius around your home. If you live in a city, five blocks may be plenty.

2. Walk out the door, stroll your streets, peruse your community, and look for anyone* who has accomplished anything you consider to be worthwhile. It could be something like achieving a dream, raising great kids, growing a happy marriage/relationship, building a successful business, graduating with good grades, beating the odds, creating a good life, remaining healthy, or simply being happy.

3. Unearth their story. Just ask them about them. Then listen deeply to what they say.

4. Now, based on the GRIT definition (above), ask yourself, "What role did *GRIT* play in this story, in their success?"

*Some of the best examples might not be the ones you search for, but the ones that land in your lap. It could be the person delivering your pizza, fixing your road, or selling you an upgrade to your cell phone package. Or it could be a friend just stopping by for a chat. If you don't feel like asking strangers, start with the people you know. Discover the impressive things it took GRIT for them to accomplish.

SPOILER ALERT: GRIT *IS* THE STORY

Every time you encounter an impressive achievement, ask, what did it take to make that happen? Scratch the surface on any significant accomplishment—you will find GRIT.

I took the GRIT Challenge. I had to. I did it to write this book. I did it to put my theories to the real test. And even after spending an entire career—thirty-five years of research, decoding and upgrading the human interface with adversity and what it takes to succeed—the GRIT Challenge frankly and fundamentally altered my entire view of both humanity and human endeavor. It moved GRIT to the top of the heap of what I coach, teach, research, parent, and strive to forever improve.

GRIT Challenge—THE REAL TEST

One day we got a call out of the blue from Celeste, the very able executive assistant for a guy who lives not far up the road. He had an unusual name: Khosro Khaloghli. Celeste had to repeat it more than once. I picked up key snippets: she said he goes by "KK" or Dr. K (whew) ... resides in a small town called Cambria.

Celeste was reaching out to my wife, Ronda, the leadership professor at Cal Poly, for her to potentially emcee an event for Dr. K and provide him some executive coaching on his presentation skills. Fun! It sounded as if he was genuinely keen on improving and mastering new skills.

As I overheard the conversation, I saw Ronda sitting up straighter and becoming more and more amazed by whatever story she was being told. And she's heard some good ones over her thirty years as a professor, which suggested this was going to be really something. So I turned on my GRIT radar and got ready to start asking questions. As soon as Ronda hung up, she turned to me, took a deep breath, and said, "Wow. You're not going to believe this one. This guy's amazing!" She was right.

KK's story begins in a one-room hovel in the poorest ghetto on the outskirts of Tehran, Iran. This is where he was born and raised. It was a hardscrabble life buried in a sandstorm of struggle, with immigrant parents who did not speak the language, and whose religion and customs were not exactly embraced.

They had nothing except whatever scraps of food they could find to feed their three children, and whatever shreds of old newspaper they could salvage to wrap Khosro's feet, so he could walk miles, often through snow, and with any luck avoid the ruthless gangs of kids on the way to school. Hungry, threatened, poor, and cold. That was how each day began and ended.

It was clear to KK, even as a very young boy, that in order to survive, he would have to learn to fend for himself. On good days when they had managed to scrape together enough money, it was his job to go stand in line for as long as two hours at the local bakery to buy a loaf of bread. Each day, as he left the shop, he was attacked by bigger kids trying to steal his bread. If he lost the scuffle, his entire family went hungry. One day, even the baker, who absentmindedly pocketed Khosro's money, accused him of not paying and beat him up, sending him home bloody and breadless.

Determined not to go home breadless anymore, KK took up wrestling, an extremely popular sport in Iran, whose wrestlers often rank among the best in the world. He knew he had to be tough to prevail in a tough world. He trained hard. He became good because he had to make it home with the bread. It was a scrappy existence. And it was all KK knew. Yet it fueled KK's determination to forge—from actual grit, mud, and dust—a better life for himself and his family. This is how his GRIT story began.

・・・・・・・・

Before I took on the GRIT Challenge, before I met "Dr. K," and before I met the tremendously diverse bunch of other gritty folks I discovered through this quest, I was convinced grit was just one of those qualities on a long list of stuff that everyone knows people need to succeed. Not really headline-making stuff. I thought it'd be kind of like having a great singing voice. Ninety-nine percent of the time, you either have it or you don't. And if you don't, you move on to or focus on something else to get your personal dose of happiness and success.

I could not have been more wrong. GRIT isn't a nice-to-have item on the get-the-most-out-of-life list. It's the single most essential item on the list. You could easily argue it IS the list. Why? Because you can't enable and enliven anything on the list without GRIT. There is no moving on or going far without it. And it can be both reliably measured and permanently improved.

GRIT is not a tattoo.

It's not like eye color or height.
It is something you can grow and change.

You can measurably improve your GRIT at any stage of life— starting now.

AQ® vs. GRIT

Think about how the role adversity—the tough stuff—plays in your success, your happiness, and your entire life. Three of my last four books have been based on the first major discovery from my thirty-five years of research: How you handle and respond to adversity is foundational to all aspects of your success.

It turns out that this thing I call your AQ® or Adversity Quotient® is tremendously predictive of your and any enterprise's performance, innovation, resilience, agility, energy, problem solving, health, and more. This has been the centerpiece of my and my firm's teachings, keynotes, coaching, programs, assessments, tools, and all the rest. I've discovered, however, that while AQ is absolutely essential, it is not sufficient. It is not enough.

THINK OF **AQ** AS *DEFENSE* AND **GRIT** AS *OFFENSE*

If AQ is all about how effectively you respond to and deal with "it"—whatever comes at you—then GRIT is about what it takes to really go for "it"—your boldest and most important goals—and make "it" happen. Defense *plus* offense. To win at anything, you pretty much need both. KK had the AQ to remain strong, but he needed and found the GRIT to forge ahead. The same can be said for anyone accomplishing uncommonly difficult and ideally worthwhile goals. GRIT creates energy, momentum, and results.

GRIT is like oxygen. It's everywhere. And anything devoid of GRIT is devoid of life. Scan life. Human life. Try *not* to find GRIT! Even though it can be pretty dormant in some people, it's in everyone and part of every meaningful achievement. It informs and fuels every great story, including yours.

How? It's simple logic. Any worthwhile, let alone *noteworthy* achievement is inherently tough. It takes considerable effort, energy, and sacrifice—usually over a significant period of time—to make it happen. Otherwise, it's not an achievement. That's GRIT. Without it, nothing happens. And it is only with it that we truly achieve. That's why you, or anyone, can benefit from not just more but also *better* GRIT.

And that's what this book is all about, helping you Grok, Gauge, and Grow both the quantity and quality of yours, so you can put its full force to your best use.

Getting to the Real Nitty-Gritty

To expand your GRIT Challenge, simply listen to or read the local news. Tune in to conversations with your friends. Use your GRIT lens like X-ray vision, to see beyond the words into the real story. GRIT is found in the happiest and the hardest stories. That's why, when you discover what makes the most fulfilled person so self-actualized, you find a story of GRIT. And that's why, in any place where you find pain and suffering, if you just scratch the surface, you're also likely to find GRIT.

 **If the person you are talking to doesn't have a good GRIT tale to tell, they know someone who does!**

I happened to be on the elevator in a medical complex, going in for a physical, and I overheard a couple of nurses talking about one of the kids in their care. "She's just so inspiring!" one commented. "I know, and she and her mom are just amazing together. I mean, did you see their hats?"

Since I had my GRIT radar on, which at this point is pretty hard to turn off, I simply said, "Sorry, I couldn't help overhearing. That girl sounds incredible. Mind if I ask what her story is?" That's how I learned about Morgan Buffaloe, of Los Osos, California. Morgan starting losing her vision when she was six. She can't see out of one eye, and is losing sight in the other. When she first felt sick, her mom took her to the doctor. They gave her ten days of antibiotics. It didn't work. She kept at it. Finally, refusing to give up, they checked her into the ER. They ran a series of tests. The CT scan revealed a brain tumor. Now this little girl is on chemo, which is making her plenty sick. But she's toughing it out, inspiring the entire staff in the process.

The motto she has embroidered on her hat?
"Wegotthis."
Morgan sums up her whole gritty mindset:
"Never stop smiling. Never give up."

Morgan and her mom are amazing. But they are far from unique. In every hospital, schoolyard, new job, single-parent home, shelter, refugee camp, natural disaster, war zone, prison, and ghetto, in any place where one must struggle, suffer, and sacrifice for a long time to make it through, we find the most stunning, elevating examples of GRIT. But who says you have to have serious hardship to spark, grow, and reap the rich rewards of GRIT?

Why wait? Why wait for some disaster to spark your GRIT, when you can enjoy and employ its full power in everything you do now?

Why This Book?

One of my main motives for writing this book is to mess with your head in a *good* way on your quest to craft an extraordinary life (business, family, team, education, relationships, etc.). I want to help you radically rethink GRIT.

You will learn:

- To understand and harness the profound upgrade from basic grit to GRIT—the comprehensive master model and mindset
- How to elevate yourself and those around you from:
  generic grit ➝ to GRIT™ ➝ to Optimal GRIT

But before we go too far, let's start with a couple of essential definitions:

GRIT: Your capacity to dig deep, to do whatever it takes—especially struggle, sacrifice, even suffer—to achieve your most worthy goals.

◯ Optimal GRIT: When you consistently and reliably demonstrate your fullest GRIT to achieve your most worthy goals.

In addition to the inspiring individual, team, and organizational examples you're about to read, I've also included several of the stories I unearthed from my GRIT Challenge, to help spark your imagination for what you might find as you continue to take on the challenge yourself. Prepare for the humbling drama and inspiring discoveries that surely await you regarding GRIT's unique potency and potential.

Why GRIT?

The GRIT Challenge—combined with the revelations I've stockpiled over the course of my life's work on the subjects of resilience, perseverance, and success—reveals Ten Basic Truths about GRIT that explain "Why *GRIT?*"—both the book and concept—and "Why now?"

1. GRIT Matters. Without it, nothing happens. Greatness suffocates. Dreams die. With it, nearly anything is possible. Humanity's finest moments arise. Ultimately, our individual and collective fates irrefutably rely upon GRIT. If you want to gauge the importance of anything, simply remove it. Picture life without it, void of its existence. Imagine:

- The all-too-common GRIT-less or GRIT-light enterprise or team, its ultimate demise brought on by its own risk aversion, collective tentativeness, fickle priorities, momentum-less meetings, and lack of fortitude
- The GRIT-less marriage, family, or partnership. If you agree that anything worth going for is inherently difficult, then, without GRIT, nothing worth going for is going to be pursued. The result? Charred remains of hope, trust, commitment, and respect haunt its barren, lifeless terrain
- The GRIT-less or GRIT-deprived child, so full of bright promise, guaranteed to prematurely and tragically dim, never to discover who or what he or she could have become, or could have contributed to a wanting world
- A GRIT-less life. The carnage of unfulfilling dreams, deflated aspirations, and discarded goals define its limp legacy. Everything worth pursuing requires a serious dose, if not a constant infusion of GRIT

2. GRIT Evolves. GRIT is like a rock you dig up with the toe of your boot on the trail. What looks at first to be minor and one-sided can be massive, deep, and multifaceted. GRIT is not just about more or less. Our most tragic and haunting failures are also generally spawned by a lack of or by the wrong brand of GRIT. GRIT is the too-often blunt, even brutish tool with which we carve our story. That's why learning the right brand and nuances of GRIT —"Smart GRIT," along with "Good GRIT" and "Strong GRIT"—is more essential than ever.

3. GRIT Trumps. On the job, GRIT has become Priority One. Ninety-eight percent of the 10,000 employers we surveyed demand it over anything else—including skills and qualifications—in the people they seek to hire, retain, invest in, and promote. It is why they would trade 7.3 "normal employees" for just one with impressive GRIT—according to more than 10,000 bosses in sixty-three countries. For GRITty leaders, it's even more.

4. GRIT Wins. New research reveals that GRIT predicts one's ability to rise up and improve one's station in life. According to Dr. Jennifer Green at University of Technology, in Sydney, grit is the overriding personal characteristic of high achievers with a disability. More generally, GRIT predicts one's ability to be gainfully employed, and at what level. It's what propels organizations, teams, and individuals to outlast, outperform, and triumph over their competition. And as MacArthur Fellow Dr. Angela Duckworth has shown, grit even predicts who wins the National Spelling Bee.

5. GRIT Ignites. Your brightest ambitions, breakthrough ideas, compelling goals, disruptive innovations, fulfilling relationships, elevating possibilities—even your best-laid, most ingenious plans—utterly depend on GRIT. And they are doomed without it. GRIT sparks and sustains the effort it takes to make things happen. You simply can't get there—you can't become who you are meant to be or contribute your finest—without a serious dose of GRIT.

6. GRIT Rules. It is the core ingredient, the fuel cell of human endeavor. The tougher things get, the more we crave and respect, revere and elevate GRIT. In a couple of brief decades, it has morphed from dim footnote to bold headline. GRIT has crescendoed from a "wanna" have to a *"gotta"* have. It so often defines our best. Right or wrong, we now view grit as a heroic and essential virtue.

7. GRIT Undergirds. It's the bedrock of relationships, progress, aspiration achievement, and results. The realization of everything and anything we strive to grow and become banks and builds on it. For any individual, team, enterprise, or culture, GRIT is what fuels the momentum, stamina, flexibility, will, strength, interdependence, agility, trust, and fortitude to endure, prevail, and win.

8. GRIT Transcends. It's vital for you, everyone you count on, and everybody you know. To the extent that it ever was, GRIT is no longer just quintessentially American. It cuts across all geographies, ages, classes, ethnicities, and cultures. That's why most of what you learn in this book will be based on worldwide, not just U.S.-based research. It's personal, communal, and universal. GRIT is bigger than and serves its potentially noble role far beyond just you and me.

9. GRIT Sticks. For years my research team and I have seen GRIT predict who stays and who quits in highly demanding jobs. Grit is also predictive of both performance and retention among teachers, as well as which cadets at West Point's first-year "Beast Barracks" are more likely to stay, bail out, or stick it out.

10. GRIT Grows. Unlike a lot of traits, GRIT can be readily understood and measured, as well as permanently improved.

Your GRIT GPS — MAPPING THE JOURNEY

GRIT is laid out in three steps at two levels. The three steps or chunks are Grok, Gauge, and Grow. You can tackle these at either the *Basic* or *Advanced* level, depending on how deep you want to go, how masterful you wish to become.

GROK—First, you need to get it

GAUGE—Next, you can assess where you are now

GROW—Then, you gain and apply the tools to improve

GROK

You will be armed with everything you need to understand and capitalize on the upgrade from traditional grit or "grit 1.0" to GRIT 2.0, or what is throughout the book referred to as simply "GRIT."

Basic Grok

You'll quickly grasp:

- The 1.0-to-2.0, grit-to-GRIT upgrade, evolution, and revolution
- G-R-I-T—The four dimensions of GRIT, what they mean, how they play out in business and life
- Robustness—The Bonus Factor—What some of history's greatest leaders teach us about what's been missing in our assessment of greatness and human endeavor, and why it can't be ignored
- The GRIT Grid Cube™—How to consider/approach GRIT from all sides

 **Use the power of *the pause*. Allow yourself to stop, reflect, and apply what you learn, in each stage of the journey.**

Advanced Grok

You'll build substantially on the basics with these additional highly practical and thought-provoking models:

- **Four Capacities**—The powerful interplay and implications of Emotional, Mental, Physical, and Spiritual GRIT

- **Situational GRIT**—Why and how GRIT can vary, along with potential upsides and downsides

- **GRIT Ladder**—The ascending rungs of GRIT, starting with you, to your relationships and teams, all the way to organizational, societal, and beyond

- **Leadership GRIT**—The role GRIT plays in what we define as and what we seek in a leader

- **Gritty Business**—Growing a gritty organization that thrives on the struggles, complexities, and uncertainties that can cripple the competition

- **Gritty Education**—Infusing GRIT as both content and method—what and *how* students learn—to fend off the mass wussification (weakening) of kids worldwide, and to retool education as the essential equipping for optimal edification and contribution for which it was (arguably) originally intended

- **Gritty Innovation**—Why GRIT, even more than grit, defines and drives putting ideas into action

- **Optimal GRIT**—Weaving all facets of GRIT into what may become your ultimate aspiration

GAUGE

You will be provided with two complimentary and complementary ways to gauge your GRIT.

Basic Gauge

The best way to dig in with the instant, fresh, powerful, and useful insights is to access the GRIT Gauge™. The GRIT Gauge has become the global gold standard— the world's preeminent online tool—for really measuring and graphing one's GRIT.

In roughly five minutes you'll see how you stack up against the global database, complete with sample profiles, provided in this book, to help you grasp the underlayers and finer implications of GRIT. This tool has been tested, selected, and implemented worldwide by the best: top leaders, athletes, institutions, and businesses—including, more recently, AT&T University (the #1-rated corporate leadership development program in the world), the highly competitive summer Launch program at MIT, coaching staff of the repeat NBA champions Miami Heat, and CEOs of some of the largest companies in the world.

This work has a deep history. As part of the research-based journey to build this, the most advanced version of the GRIT Gauge, my PEAK Team and I have measured and strengthened the key elements of GRIT in more than a million people in thousands of companies, schools, and organizations across sixty-three countries over the past three and a half decades.

Advanced Gauge

To help you rise up to the Advanced level, I am providing you the opportunity to complete as much of the GRIT Mix Assessment as you care to take on. You'll be in good company. You'll tackle some of the same questions and challenges I've presented to Harvard Business School for their MBA and Executive Education programs, as well as to the trenches of the corporate world.

If you're not a corporate type, global leader, or an aspiring entrepreneur, don't sweat it, and don't stop reading! These are also the same tools offered up to wounded warriors in the military, disadvantaged populations, and students of all ages, in schools and universities around the world. It has helped parents raising kids, couples facing divorce, people relocating for or seeking a new job, and so much more. In short, it's stuff almost anyone can take on and wrestle with to Grow their GRIT.

The GRIT Mix Assessment is a much more comprehensive look at every angle and facet of your GRIT. It both builds directly and expands significantly upon what you learned from your GRIT Gauge experience. Through the GRIT Mix Assessment you will quickly come to terms with your current blend of GRIT-related tendencies, strengths, weak spots, and opportunities, compared to what the ideal Optimal GRIT Mix for you might be.

GROW

Grow equips you with a series of proven, honed, world-tested tools for measurably enhancing your GRIT. Many of these are the same tools used in the live sessions conducted by me and members of my PEAK Team.

Basic Grow

These Basic tools set you up with easy ways to upgrade GRIT with anyone, in any context, starting with yourself.

- WhyTry™—An instant, practical tool for gauging and creating optimal alignment between motivation and effort at individual, team, and organizational levels
- GRIT Goads™—G-R-I-T-specific, tested questions for getting immediate traction within yourself and with others

Advanced Grow

These Advanced tools help you take a more holographic approach to upgrading your and others' GRIT, to make it (and you) consistently stronger, smarter, and "gooder" across all situations.

- Gritty Goals—Quickest tool for creating the kind of goals worth going for
- The Gritty Game Plan—Add GRIT to your entire strategy and approach
- GRIT Gang—Simple two-step tool for harnessing the contagious power of Secondhand GRIT

It's important to reiterate that all of these tools are based on research and application forged by my PEAK Team and top-flight independent researchers through our work across sixty-three countries, thousand of companies, and more than a million individuals. Based on real data and often-unsolicited feedback, these tools have enriched countless lives, relationships, families, careers, teams, and organizations, even societies.

Philosophy and Approach

After facilitating a recent GRIT session at MIT, one of the esteemed hosts commented, "Now I get it, Dr. Paul. You're more of a practical nerd." I could think of no finer compliment!

Practically Obsessed. This book and all of my work are based on the same basic obsession: "If you can't put it to real, meaningful, and immediate use, what's the point?" Really. I want this book to move your head and heart, and to ultimately fortify your entire life. If you run a business, I want it to fuel your bottom line and your ultimate success in taking on and achieving bold, worthy ambitions.

No Rules. This is your book. Pick and choose whatever you need. Skip around all you like. I'd love to see you go after GRIT like your first real, nutritious meal in a long time. Do whatever it takes to suck the marrow out of the bone. You may even decide to come back for seconds, or to share. I hope you do.

Impact Is Everything. All I care about is helping you move toward living, and ideally becoming an exemplar of, Optimal GRIT. You'll learn exactly what that means and entails. Because you, as an individual, can spawn grittier relationships, teams, organizations, and societies—the stuff that changes the world. More of the right kind of GRIT can do a lot of good.

Go and Do vs. Academic Review. It's important to clarify what *GRIT* is not. It's not an academic compendium. Coming at this with the goal of being simple, succinct, and practical creates tough trade-offs.

Titrating down to a few simple models, measures, and tools from the roughly 2,500 studies in all the grit-related research, including our own decades of independent studies, was not an easy—although an essential—task. And trust me, by fashioning this book as more of a portable field guide than a scholarly tome, I've utterly failed to do justice to the lifetimes of inquiry or brilliance that support much of what I've offered up in *GRIT*. The PEAK Team and I continue to conduct independent studies with help from top experts at the Educational Testing Service, to advance the pure nerd side as well.

Bring It On! This book represents a giant and immensely fulfilling chunk of my life. Even so, it is most definitely also a work in progress. GRIT is evolving, quickly and steadily. So, I'm approaching it with pretty much an open source code mindset. I'd be immensely grateful for any stories, questions, challenges, frustrations, revelations, applications, and ideally, improvements you wish to offer me at *paul@peaklearning.com,* or my team at *info@peaklearning.com.*

Ultimately, I hope to help you enjoy in your life what this work has brought to mine, which is a rich sense of "gritification," that cellular-level fulfillment that only comes from fighting long and hard to achieve something terribly difficult and worthwhile. Dig deep, apply what you learn in these pages, and I believe you'll be gritified too.

GROK: To understand something profoundly and intuitively

This section has one overarching purpose—to help you *GROK,* really understand, the basics of *GRIT*, which you began to unearth in the GRIT Challenge. "Grok" is an uncomfortable, awkward term. That's intentional. Grok goes beyond knowing, understanding, even remembering. It's like an infusion. It's a revelation and realization that changes you. It's the highest level of understanding. This level of understanding is the essential foundation to both Gauge and Grow your GRIT, from which you can ascend to the Advanced level, if you choose.

 **To get the most out of this section, ask yourself, who has not only the most, but also the best GRIT? What makes it "best"?**

Grokking begins with looking at grit 1.0 vs. GRIT 2.0, and why GRIT is actually multidimensional. I'll explain the four dimensions of GRIT, along with the Bonus Factor, the element missing from the generic approach to grit. You will then Grok the GRIT Cube to comprehend and consider GRIT more holographically, shaping your pathway to Optimal GRIT.

grit 1.0

Grit is hot. It goes beyond a trend. In case you somehow missed the headlines over the past few years, grit has hit big in popular media, and has swiftly spread far and wide as the latest trend in education and parenting. Grit's also become an essential element of corporate training, leadership development, and sales.

Grit's the new buzzword. And as a result, it often gets misunderstood, loosely used, and watered down. That's the downside. Beyond our work and research over the past couple of decades, the positive upside of this trend has been largely led by the aforementioned top-flight research conducted by MacArthur grant-winning professor Angela Duckworth and her esteemed colleagues.

To date, these other researchers' straightforward and basic approach to grit has been focused on the *quantity* or degree of grit that individuals—primarily students, cadets, and teachers—say they have. They ask, "How much grit do you have?" And it begs the question, "Can a person have too much grit?"

With this book, and based on the realities and limitations I have witnessed in real-world application of grit 1.0, I would respectfully like to expand, perhaps redefine that focus to achieve a more holographic and immediately practical explanation, method, and toolset for actually growing all aspects of GRIT. Here's the difference, and the upgrade I propose.

Over these past decades of doing GRIT-related research and application, I have come to believe—and my research has resoundingly confirmed—that grit, *true grit*, is about much more than quantity. In fact, *quality* can matter more. It's not about having the most, but also showing the *best* GRIT. And, research again indicates, it's about more than basic consistency and persistence. Quantity, vs. quantity AND quality. That's the upgrade from "grit" to "GRIT."

> **...grit, true grit, is about much more than quantity. In fact, *quality* can matter more. It's not about having the most, but also showing the *best* GRIT.**

GRIT 2.0

"GRIT" refers to "GRIT 2.0." It represents the scientifically grounded, research-based, practicality-obsessed upgrade from grit 1.0. GRIT 2.0—it is the focus of this entire book and why I use GRIT throughout the remainder. GRIT 2.0 introduces you and the rest of the world to the first-ever hybrid of quantity *and* quality of GRIT. It asks not just, "How much GRIT do you have?" but also provides insight into "What kind of GRIT do you have and show?" Or, more specifically, "To what extent do you demonstrate the best kind of GRIT, in the right situations, with the right people, in the right ways?"

- GRIT 2.0 puts you on a path to *Optimal GRIT*. It provides entirely new, rich, practical insights into parts of you and your personal equation for success you might not even have known you had

- GRIT 2.0 is made up of four building blocks, G-R-I-T. It also includes a bonus factor, which has to do with the wear and tear GRIT can cause, over time

- GRIT 2.0 is gauged and grown along three axes: Strong/Weak, Good/Bad, and Smart/Dumb

- GRIT 2.0 is applied across situations and at all levels of your potential impact or contribution

- GRIT 2.0 provides a high-def and 3-D perspective

grit 1.0 = "grit" (quantity)

GRIT 2.0 = "GRIT" (Quantity + Quality)

GRIT 2.0—as you Grok, Gauge, and Grow these facets of your GRIT, you will find yourself demonstrating stronger, "gooder," and smarter GRIT, across a broader spectrum of situations, with some soul-stirring, potentially game-changing results.

FOUR⁺ DIMENSIONS OF GRIT

GRIT is about more than sheer tenacity or perseverance. It's more than just sticking with a goal. When you dig deeper, when you peel back its simple veneer, you quickly realize that *true* GRIT is also made of energy, effort, dedication, agility, perspective, and fortitude. GRIT also has a lot to do with what *you do* with adversity.

Research validates what your instincts have probably already figured out about the guts of GRIT. There are four building blocks that form and fuel your GRIT. These are the same four building blocks that we've been teaching, gauging, and growing in tens of thousands of people worldwide. Each of these dimensions stands on its own feet, statistically, and each contributes to the overall GRIT™ construct.

G ROWTH

Your propensity to seek and consider new ideas, additional alternatives, different approaches, and fresh perspectives.

R ESILIENCE

Your capacity to respond constructively and ideally make good use of all kinds of adversity.

I NSTINCT

Your gut-level capacity to pursue the right goals in the best and smartest ways.

T ENACITY

The degree to which you persist, commit to, stick with, and relentlessly go after whatever you choose to achieve.

GROWTH
Your propensity to seek and consider new ideas, additional alternatives, different approaches, and fresh perspectives.

"If we only did things that were easy, we wouldn't actually be learning anything. We'd just be practicing things we already knew."

— DAVID DOCKTERMAN, CHIEF ARCHITECT, LEARNING SCIENCES AT SCHOLASTIC EDUCATION; ADJUNCT LECTURER AT THE HARVARD GRADUATE SCHOOL OF EDUCATION

Growth is a mindset. When James Reed and I set out to write the book *Put Your Mindset to Work,* our research, including a series of independent studies, showed Growth to be a pivotal element of GRIT, and of a winning mindset, overall.

"Mindset" has long been a pretty flabby, nebulous term. It's lacked firmness and definition. People use it interchangeably with—or as the updated term for—"attitude," when in fact mindset is so much more. It goes much deeper than attitude. It is actually the lens through which you see and navigate life.

The more James and I heard people loosely tossing around the terms "mindset" or "right mindset," the more determined we became that the time had come to truly define what comprises what we called a "winning mindset." It was time to find out if it even mattered. We had to discover, once and for all, what, if any, dimensions of mindset really make a measurable difference in someone's prospects and success.

Mindset.
The lens through which you see and navigate life.

In partnership with a top researcher from the Educational Testing Service in Princeton, New Jersey, we first compiled a master list of everything any scholar, expert, and researcher suggested might matter when it comes to mindset. Second, we asked thousands of top employers and tens of thousands of leaders worldwide to rank order those items in terms of importance. We then went through a series of iterations—testing and tweaking, testing and tweaking— in the way we measured mindset.

Not only were we able to create a firm definition and model of a winning mindset, we also discovered that GRIT, overall, is the fuel cell of all the other elements. Without it, nothing much happens. There are, however, particular dimensions of mindset that make a real difference in what you achieve and who you become.

Growth is one of those dimensions. Carol Dweck, professor of psychology at Stanford University, pioneered the original, pivotal research separating the difference between what is called a "fixed" vs. "growth" mindset.

The majority of Dweck's work has focused on children and students. Her groundbreaking efforts have shown that those who believe intelligence or talent to be fixed tend to give up more easily than those who believe that, through effort, talent and ability can be learned and improved.

Our research with adults, both working and unemployed, has shown similar results. Those with a Growth mindset are statistically more likely to get, keep, engage in, and succeed at work. Growth matters. This single dimension of mindset affects their GRIT, which is why it is the first dimension of the master model—based on our original and ensuing research—GRIT.

But our definition has a twist. It goes beyond "fixed" vs. "growth" in the standard sense. We discovered that one's propensity to seek and/or consider different alternatives, perspectives, approaches, and/or opinions has a significant effect on one's ability to forge ahead effectively toward one's goals. So, with all due respect to Dr. Dweck and her esteemed team, at least in our analyses with people like you, this expanded definition is proving to be more predictive and powerful.

To recap our definition of Growth: *Your propensity to seek and consider new ideas, additional alternatives, different approaches, and fresh perspectives.*

KK *KK had always wanted to go to school, to attend the university. He had a ferociously inquisitive mind. But his family had no money. And his father passed away, leaving KK's sister and mother dependent on whatever money KK would bring home. As a young man, he was at a dead end, with no clear future.*

So, as a teenager, he did the unheard of. He went to work as a roughneck in the oil fields in the middle of the desert, working with men twice his age. He had to learn from scratch. It was brutal, exhausting, and dangerous work. People were injured every day, and according to KK, "People are killed all the time."

The heat among the wind-whipped sands would regularly reach 110–120 degrees, or more. You worked twenty-one straight days, with one week off. It paid well, because so few men could handle the conditions and do the work.

As physically grueling as the work was, it was more emotionally trying for KK as his dreams seemed to move further and further away.

"One of the most painful things to me was going into town on my week off. I would get on the bus with all those university students, who were dressed nice and carrying their briefcases, and think, 'What makes them better than me? Why do they get to go and not me? Why can't I get an education too?' I felt like second-class citizen. It hurt me very deeply. I was determined not to spend my life feeling this way."

The youngest roughneck by far, KK was given the worst shifts and the ugliest jobs. But he stuck it out for seven years, earning the respect of one of the American bosses, who convinced KK he needed to find his way to America, or he would never give his family a better life. KK constantly sought the American's insights, advice, and wisdom.

Since student visas and work visas could not be had, he took his mentor's advice and split the money he had saved up with his mother, so she and his sister could eat while he went to America on a three-month visitor visa. It was a big risk, because the visitor visa expressly prohibited him from working or studying once he landed in America.

He took the cheapest flight, landing in the United States thirty hours later. "I arrived in Los Angeles airport at midnight. Everyone had someone there greeting them. I knew no one. I did not speak any English, I had $300 in my pocket, and I had no plan. I just knew I had to make it work for my family. I was twenty-four years old."

So, KK hailed a taxi and blurted his best attempt at two words in his thick accent: "Cheap motel." The driver took him to some fleabag hotel, which cost $12 per night. It was a fortune in KK's world. And it was a wake-up call. Clearly his money would not last.

The next day, he kicked his Growth mindset into high gear. He knew he was out of his element, and that he would have to ask a lot of people a lot of questions to get the answers he needed. The questions started when he went to the front desk and said another word, "school," asked how to get there, and was given directions and bus routes to get to UCLA. When he stumbled onto campus, again he asked anyone he could find for directions and help, with whatever broken words and gestures he could muster, until someone helped him land in the Foreign Students office.

Once he was there, he asked more questions. It was at the Foreign Students office that he met an Iranian student working on a class schedule. KK could now ask questions in Farsi, his native tongue. The student told KK that since, due to his visitor visa, he was forbidden from enrolling in school, his only chance might be an open enrollment wrestling tournament that was coming up in a week. "The guy told me that if I could win, the coaches would do everything to get me a student visa, and I could stay. I knew if I worked hard enough, I could win."

Although he had not been training, KK signed up. At the tournament, there was a famous wrestler who was very tough. KK was told, "Beat that guy, and you stay. Lose, and you go home." It was the match of his life.

As KK describes it, "I do not know what happened. I just know I won. I think I was so sick from being so exhausted that I blacked out. But I got to stay. I went to university. And it was there they gave me a job, as an assistant coach, so I could send money to my family. When you are lost, when you have to find a way, you have to ask people questions. Find smart people. Get their ideas. This is what I had to do. This is the only way to make things happen."

· · · · · · ·

Growth is what helps get you unstuck. KK had been just another poor, uneducated kid who seemed destined to be stuck doing what to him was pretty meaningless work. Everyone and everything around him told him to accept his fate. No way out. But rather than myopically digging that rut even deeper, he possessed the GRIT to lift his eyes, scan his world, and ask the right Growth-minded questions to develop some powerful options; questions like, "What don't I know that I need to know? Whom can I ask to get the answers I need? What not-immediately obvious, alternative angles or approaches should I consider?" These and other upcoming, Growth-related questions help people like KK look beyond and rise above.

> "I learn new things; I ask lots of questions.
> It's a practice. I'm responsible to answer all the questions.
> At the end of the day, everybody comes to me.
> I have to put my mind to work to find the answer."
> — KHOSRO KHALOGHLI, REAL ESTATE DEVELOPER

In your opinion, how likely is a guy like KK to make a real difference? Despite what was once his dead-end destiny, would you bet on him to contribute meaningfully to the world? Notice, while his words are simple, the path was tough. It takes GRIT, and it takes Growth to transform your destiny.

RESILIENCE

Your capacity to respond constructively to—and ideally make good use of—all kinds of adversity.

"You may not control all the events that happen to you, but you can decide not to be reduced by them."
— MAYA ANGELOU, CIVIL RIGHTS ACTIVIST, POET, AUTHOR

What happens inside you when adversity strikes? And what exactly *is* adversity? If we define adversity as, "When you predict or experience something bad happening to someone or something you care about," you can immediately see just how personal this adversity thing can be.

Adversity.

When you predict or experience something bad happening to someone or something you care about.

You can break adversity down into its two main parts. First, *how bad do you perceive it to be?* If it's potentially tragic or cataclysmic, it might score a ten. If it's really nothing, it might be a zero or one, on the ten-point Adversity Scale. People often differ in their perceptions. That's why when someone else is having a meltdown over something, even in your most empathic moments, you may be privately thinking, "What's the big deal?" To them it's a ten. To you, it's a one. How bad is it? That's Part One.

Part Two is, *how much do you really care?* Traffic jams always provide a ripe example. To the executive running late for a board meeting or the factory worker who could be disciplined for being late, it's major stress. To the elderly man who prefers the slower speeds and is taking his sweet time to go to the drugstore, it's hardly an inconvenience, and may be a relief.

What exactly is resilience? A new house paint has recently hit the market with a smartly designed label spelling out its superior value proposition in one word, "Resilience," promising to be "Great, no matter what the forecast." It is apparently concocted to withstand moisture better than its competitors. In short, it promises to hold up better and longer in wet weather. Not a bad characteristic—for a paint. But for us humanoids, resilience can mean, and we can *use* it to be, so much more.

Resilience can and should go way beyond simply bouncing back from adversity. Human resilience is your capacity to respond constructively to—to be strengthened and improved by—adversity. With this definition, adversity becomes fuel, to elevate and propel you to places you could never get to without it.

Resilience.
Your capacity to respond constructively to—to be strengthened and improved by—adversity.

What's your personal relationship with adversity? Like most people, do you respond better to some stuff than other stuff? Do you handle the bigger challenges better than the smaller ones? Or is it the other way around? What if you could become more "Response Able," able to respond more effectively, to more things, more quickly? Imagine the effect this would have on your peace of mind, your confidence, and your will to persevere.

It's nearly impossible to imagine, but back in the early '90s when my team and I introduced our AQ® (Adversity Quotient®) theory and method to the world, almost no one had heard of the word "resilience." Each time we mentioned it, we had to explain what it meant. Today, in this post-9/11, intertwined, and uncertain world, the word "resilience" or "resilient" is used to describe everything from athletes to car seats, household brooms to cheap perfumes, hair spray to the words leaders say. Resilience is everywhere.

Parents and teachers are supposed to grow resilient kids. We want resilient financial portfolios and banking institutions to better weather the next crisis. Organizations are supposed to provide resilience training to help their people thrive in difficult times. And, at times, it seems every trainer, consultant, and facilitator out there has rebranded himself or herself around it, or at least added "resilience" to their quiver of offerings.

What if you could become more "Response Able," able to respond more effectively, to more things, more quickly? Imagine the effect this would have on your *peace of mind, your confidence, and your will to persevere.*

KK *Soon after transferring schools to complete his degree in Urban Planning at California State Polytechnic University at Pomona, KK discovered that gasoline prices were skyrocketing at the pumps from twenty-three to thirty-seven cents per gallon. Gas stations were closing left and right, convinced that people were going to stop driving and stop buying fuel. But KK saw the opportunity in the adversity.*

He took the money he had scraped together from odd jobs and began buying stations, one by one, very cheap. He was determined to turn adversity into an advantage. But he knew he had to find people who shared his mindset to turn these abandoned businesses into gold. It's hard to create a resilient business without resilient people.

For each of his managers, he cut the same deal, splitting the profits 50-50. "I always trust my heart, my gut. I look for people who have that thing; they are not afraid to dig deep, work hard. They have to be hungry. The best ones have usually faced some adversity."

One of his best hires of all time was Roy. "This was a big station. Important station. And here were all these guys coming applying for the job—fat, smoking, sloppy, lazy. They'd say, 'I have twenty years' experience running service station.' I'd think, 'Yeah, so you go out front, smoke, and greet my customers looking like that, with your hands on your hips while they pump their own gas? No way!'"

He continues: "Then up drives this guy. Big burly guy. He has his pregnant wife and child in the truck, and leaves them so he can come talk to me. So, on the application form, he only fills in his name. I ask him to fill in his experience, background, etc. He says, 'I didn't do that, because if I did, you wouldn't hire me.'"

"Why not?" KK asked.

"Because I just got out of prison. Seven years. But I did my time, and now, as you can see (he gestures toward his wife), I really need a job. I promise you. No one will work harder than me."

"So, I said, 'You're hired.' I hired him on the spot. He worked so hard, took so much pride. His wife would come by with their kids, and they'd be polishing the pumps, to make them shine brighter. I hired him because he had been through adversity, and he was hungry for a better life."

Using this formula, and fueled by his resilience and the resilience of others, KK revived dozens of ailing gas stations into thriving businesses, and built his first of many empire-from-the-ashes successes. That's not coping with or overcoming adversity. We call that <u>harnessing</u> adversity, the higher form of resilience.

INSTINCT

Your gut-level capacity to pursue the right goals in the best and smartest ways.

"You have to really be courageous about your instincts and your ideas. Otherwise you'll just knuckle under, and things that might have been memorable will be lost."
— FRANCIS FORD COPPOLA, FILM DIRECTOR, PRODUCER, SCREENWRITER

This one's tough, utterly essential, and it's been uniformly missing from the entire conversation on grit. It's also immensely humbling. How much energy, time, effort, hope, and resources have you expended pursuing the wrong stuff, or pursuing the right stuff in the wrong ways? For most people the answer is, "A heck of a lot." Some classic examples include:

- Taking advice from the wrong person on your academic major
- Stubbornly negotiating a deal based on what you think they want, not what they really want
- Repeatedly trying to win over someone whose not even good for you
- Killing yourself trying to complete a task or solve a problem at work, only to discover it's the wrong one
- Spending hours on the phone with the airlines, your cable company, or some service provider, only to find out you could resolve the problem within five minutes by yourself, online
- Beating yourself up for a weakness or need, rather than getting help
- Desperately trying to get your child to do something in a way that completely backfires
- Staying in the "fast lane" on the freeway, when the other lanes are clearly moving faster
- Leading or influencing others by repeatedly using the wrong levers or appeals

I recently asked this question of 350 top telecom executives, and their answer was, "More than half." More than half their time, effort, resources, energy, and more were spent pursuing less-than-optimal goals, in less-than-optimal ways. No wonder their stock has been comparatively mired for the past few years.

But before we pretend to be aghast at their inefficiency or lack of clarity and discipline, it's important to point out that their answer is entirely normal. Based on my team's research, they are on par with the numbers and proportions provided by leaders across all industries, worldwide.

That's just business. Imagine a human life. Your life. What proportion of *your* energy, effort, hope, resources, and time has been and is being spent pursuing less-than-optimal goals, and/or in less-than-optimal ways?

Put another way, how many of your goals would you say are absolutely optimal, meaning they could not be more right, more on target, more important? Oh, and add to that this question: What proportion of your strategies and approaches toward any goals would you consider optimal, meaning they honestly could not be any more effective, on the mark, efficient, smart, or better?

The brutal but compelling truth is that it's impossible to lead an optimal life or grow an optimal business without developing the Instinct to pursue optimal goals in optimal ways. Of course no one ever does this 100 percent of the time. But significantly increasing the proportion of your goals and strategies that are increasingly close to optimal is what the whole GRIT game, and this brief journey, is all about.

The other brutal truth is, most people spend a meaningful chunk of their time pursuing less-than-meaningful endeavors, in less-than-optimal ways. How many people do you see or know who have clearly hardwired themselves to obsessively check and respond to texts and emails, regardless of whatever more important events may be stirring around them? Ron Friedman, Ph.D., brings this to light in his recent *Harvard Business Review* blog, "The Cost of Continuously Checking Email," in which he makes it clear that our email compulsion is the efficiency equivalent of rushing to the store every time you run low on a single item. The point being, there is a better, smarter way to go at it and to get stuff done.

GRIT Challenge—USING YOUR INSTINCTS

If you've ever seen a television show called Deadliest Catch, it gives you a small sense of what Bob Dooley has undauntedly taken on for the past forty years of his life. For thirty-three of those years, he was a skipper of a fishing boat in the frigid winter waters of the Bering Sea.

How do you stay alive, keep your crew alive, keep your boat running, keep your marriage intact, let alone make any money, when you are out at sea 24/7, operating mostly in the dark, in some of toughest waters in the world, for up to 120 days at a time, with almost no way to communicate with your loved ones back home? And what role does Instinct play?

I asked Bob what he had faced in a typical trip. "The main thing was, you never knew what was going to happen. We could head out, face one hundred-mile-per-hour winds, with temperatures so cold the spray freezes on the deck, which is pretty dangerous, because if the ice builds, it can roll your boat and you're sunk. Your gear is constantly failing or breaking, so you have to make repairs on the fly. We invent new ways to do stuff all the time."

When I asked him for an example, he said, "Oh, there are countless examples. One time, we were heading out in a terrible storm. We had to. We had to make money. We knew we had to catch some fish. The headwind was ninety knots, and the waves pretty big, like fifty-foot, and one big breaker busted out one of the big windows in the wheelhouse. Half the electrical in the boat died. Water was gushing in. And we're talking cold water. We were in trouble."

I asked him what he did. "We did what you do every day at sea. You have to constantly reassess your goal, your situation, and your plan. In this case, we patched the hole with a big buoy, got rid of what water we could, secured the situation, and limped back to shore. And it's not like a lot of these problems get solved quickly, then life is good. That's not how it works out there. When we got ashore at 2 a.m., there was nowhere to dock. We made what repairs we could. The caulk in the window couldn't even dry. But we had to head back out. It took thirty-six hours in those conditions to go what normally took twelve. And that was just the start of our trip."

"You gotta fight through adversity. But you can't just fight. That's why they gave us opposable thumbs. So we can do it smart. You gotta use your instincts to make the right moves, and reroute when you have to. If you don't, you're dead."

— BOB DOOLEY, BOAT CAPTAIN, OWNER, CONSULTANT, ADVISOR, INDUSTRY EXPERT

Starting with nothing, and after losing everything, Bob rebuilt his enterprise into one of the more successful, and certainly among the most respected, on the seven seas. He now serves as one of the world's leading experts on the fishing industry, being called upon to testify before the U.S. Congress and advise policy makers. His efforts have helped pioneer the best practices on fishery management and sustainability that secure a vital element of the world's food supply. Not bad for a scrappy kid working the crab stand at his mother's store.

Instinct is deceptive. Stoney, my cattle-herding dog, has an innate drive to relentlessly chase animals. But his ability to go after the right ones in the most efficient and effective manner has been largely learned. Likewise, while you possess some base-level GRIT Instinct, it can be significantly developed and honed. It's encouraging to see what the research reveals: You can readily strengthen your Instinct, pursuing even more optimal goals, in even more effective ways at any age or stage of life. Awareness, or Grokking, is the first step. Applying GRIT tools, real-time, to Grow GRIT comes next.

TENACITY

The degree to which you persist, commit to, stick with, and relentlessly work at whatever you choose to achieve.

"A wedding anniversary is the celebration of love, trust, partnership, tolerance, and tenacity. The order varies for any given year."
— PAUL SWEENEY, AUTHOR

Resilience without Tenacity helps keep you whole, but it only goes so far. Tenacity propels you across the finish line. How many attempts, how many starts and stops, how many heartfelt efforts over how much time does it take to break through and succeed? After all these decades of studying and applying Tenacity, I still don't know how to answer this question, except to say, "One more."

If most grand quests take longer and are more difficult than originally imagined, Tenacity is what determines the difference between scoring a fail or the (Holy) Grail. As you will soon discover, however, not all Tenacity is good, effective, noble, or even sane. Sometimes it creates a palpable "uh-oh" feeling.

You've no doubt either been or known someone who, at least for a period of time, pushes beyond what other, more "reasonable" minds would consider prudent. Perhaps you've been on the receiving or participatory end of the whispers, rumors, and/or jokes that are often shared at the expense of, or at least to covertly describe someone who's gone Frankenstein—clearly tipped to the dark side—or simply gone too far.

It turns out that nearly all major breakthroughs, innovations, and step changes in history took seemingly senseless levels of Tenacity. They required sticking with it long after other, "saner," less determined people would have tossed in the towel.

> *"I think it would be great to be born on Earth and to die on Mars.*
> *Just hopefully not at the point of impact."*
>
> **— ELON MUSK, CEO AND CTO OF SPACEX, CEO AND CHIEF PRODUCT**
> **ARCHITECT OF TESLA MOTORS, AND CHAIRMAN OF SOLARCITY**

KK *Before he could ever afford his first gas station, KK had to find a way to make more money to send to his family in Iran. No job was beneath him. So, he jumped at the chance to earn a few bucks as a lifeguard at the local pool. He did what gritty people everywhere do: He distinguished himself by going above and beyond the job description. He cleaned the pool, painted the*

lifeguard chair, did all the least desirable jobs, which he attacked with his customary GRIT. "You go early. You clean good, better than any one. You get down on your knees and you scrub. Hard. You make it the cleanest pool anyone has ever seen. Every day. Day after day. You never miss. And once you earn their respect, only then you can ask for more."

Khosro Khaloghli—from lifeguard to pool manager and swimming instructor.

He noticed that there were down times at the pool. "So, I went to the boss and I say, 'Why don't you give lessons? Teach kids and their parents to be swimmers?'" Since he had his water safety and lifeguard certifications, KK taught the lessons. His reputation as the best teacher grew. Due to his initiative with cleaning the pool and teaching lessons, the owners put him in charge of all the pools. KK used his tenacity to improve his situation.

Tenacity is what is required of anyone trying to rise above tough circumstances. In fact, this is one of the factors GRIT actually predicts. James Ward is only nineteen years old and for the past five years has been homeless in Skid Row Los Angeles, moving between shelters, switching from school to school, and living in his mother's car. Despite his dismal existence, but compelled by the dream of a college-spurred better life for him and his family, he somehow found a way to dig deep, stay focused to keep his grades up, and to help his siblings to do the same. Despite all the pervasive crime, grime, fear, poverty, uncertainty, instability, hunger, and hopelessness, James found a way to persevere and successfully graduate from San Pedro High School—his third school in four years.

Graduating was only his first daunting goal. Getting into and paying for college seemed, in many ways, even more unattainable. He applied for a Parent PLUS Loan and was denied. But despite all the odds and compassionate naysayers, he refused to give up. Clearly, traditional funding wouldn't work.

When formerly homeless Jessica Sutherland, a junior producer at Yahoo! Studios, spoke at James' school, he did something very gritty. He immediately approached her, asked for her email address, and reached out to her before she made it home. He asked for help. That can be an important part of not just Tenacity, but Growth as well. The average cost to attend Howard University is $32,165, plus another $12,000–$14,000 for books, supplies, transportation, and incidentals.

So together Jessica and James launched an online campaign called "Homeless to Howard." Within a week they gathered $12,000 in donations, and his relentless efforts resulted in some additional loans and grants. He entered Howard University in the fall of 2014 as the first member of his family ever to attend college.

"I want to be an astrophysicist or an engineer," said Ward, setting his sights high. "But it was never about me. It was always about my younger brother and sister learning that education is what they need, because as long as you have knowledge, no one can ever take it from you."

> "FEARLESS is getting back up and fighting for what you want over and over again … even though every time you've tried before, you've lost."
>
> — TAYLOR SWIFT, SINGER-SONGWRITER, BEST-SELLING DIGITAL MUSIC ARTIST

Surprisingly, some people really hold back from showing or tapping their Tenacity, keeping it in a vault, as if saving it for a particular crisis. So, while it's true, some do appear to possess greater overall Tenacity than others, the bigger question is, how much of the Tenacity and GRIT you have are you willing to bring, especially when it really counts? Most people would bet on the person with modest Tenacity, who brings 100 percent of it into play, vs. a person possessing a greater amount, but displays little or none when the game is on.

KK *As you hope to make happen with any and all dimensions of GRIT, sometimes Instinct and Tenacity meld together. Beginning with the service stations, the more KK's success as a real estate developer grew, the more he knew he had to lose. When the recession of the 1980s hit, and interest rates skyrocketed to 22 percent, he knew he couldn't keep going on the same path. He had to reroute.*

So, he flew to Vietnam. He knew, with all the rebuilding they had to do, that they would need some basic materials. He laughs, "It was second time, like landing in LA, when I came to America. Hah! I land. I know no one. I speak no Vietnamese. I have no plan. But I know I will make something happen. Always."

Being a disciplined guy, he stayed in a cheap hotel to save money, but spent the $8 to work out at another hotel's gym every day. He was trying to find his way in a land of complete unknowns. The gym gave him the stability and familiarity he needed.

It was there that a random Australian guy approached him and said, "Are you KK?" Khosro was shocked.

"How can you know me?"

"I saw you in Men's Fitness *magazine! Amazing photos!" That sparked a conversation about the construction situation in Vietnam, which led KK to reroute his investments and efforts by purchasing a gravel business.*

"It's not that hard. [This is a frequent comment by people with exceptional GRIT.] You just have to look, use your head, and ask yourself, 'How can I make this better?' They had many broken trucks. They only worked one shift. And it was very inefficient. So, I added lights, I bought new trucks, I improved the situation. I made it more efficient. We increased production by ten times where it was. We gave so many people good jobs. We gave them hope."

I asked him how it worked out, and he got that signature gleam in his eyes. "Pretty well!" he boomed. I asked how well. "I sold it for forty times the price I paid, two and a half years later."

THE BONUS FACTOR—ROBUSTNESS

How well you hold up—the degree to which you are worn down or become stronger—over time.

Abraham Lincoln and Winston Churchill. Two historic heroes who had grit and resilience figured out, right? Not exactly. When you scrutinize both men, something's out of whack. Both suffered from abject, crippling depression—what Churchill called his "black dog," and Lincoln referred to as "hypo" (short for hypochondriasis).

Most psychologists have been trained to believe that the traditional definitions of resilience and grit both reside at opposite ends of the psychological hardiness spectrum from melancholia.

That is why enhanced resilience and grit are commonly the depression-reducing ambitions and strategies of choice and why some of the largest training investments in human history are based on this conclusion.

However, both of these depression-prone, world-changing leaders were able to A) make a lifetime of momentous contributions, while B) having no apparent loss of GRIT along the way. The missing factor that explains this mystery appears to be their Robustness. It is both the reason and the result.

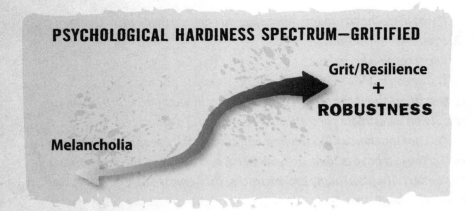

PSYCHOLOGICAL HARDINESS SPECTRUM—GRITIFIED

Grit/Resilience
+
ROBUSTNESS

Melancholia

Robustness is both gradual and dramatic. On one hand, it is the accumulated, positive or negative, day-by-day effect of one's entire life experience. On the other hand, it spells the difference between a victorious and tragic life. If it took everything you have to get to where you are—all your optimism, life force, effort, talent, and resources—leaving you an utterly drained shell of your former self, that's likely irrevocable. Whether or not such martyrdom is necessary or heroic is determined by what was at stake, what alternatives (if any) existed, and what you achieved.

Through my three and a half decades of research, I've discovered something simple and profound. Over the course of your life, it comes down to one of two things. Either adversity consumes you, or you consume it. Either life wears and beats you down, or it fortifies and/or energizes you.

Unfortunately, the first reality is far more common, to the point that we might even call it "a normal human life." For many people, their GRIT wears down like cheap sandpaper. What once had bite, grip, and effect becomes ineffective. They become worn gritless by the tests of time, leaving little of what's required to attack the next endeavor. There's nothing noble about unnecessarily beating oneself to a bloody pulp in the pursuit of living a worthy life.

Aging, in and of itself, naturally diminishes certain capacities. The speed and degree of such loss appears, for most people, to be largely negotiable. That's why most people, beyond merely aging, become diminished in important ways by life's vicissitudes.

A rare few do not. Not only do they hold up, they also become what the hard-core bodybuilders at the gym call "juiced and jacked" or "stoked and yoked." They are overtly or covertly stronger and more on fire because of the grit they have shown and grown along the way. They are at the upper end of the bell curve on Robustness. In comparison to their grit-worn counterparts, they can therefore much more fully enjoy whatever rich rewards of life they have achieved and earned to get to where they are.

This becomes especially apparent with time. Time cannot lie. That's why Robustness—the wear-and-tear factor—is so undeniable.

KK *I cannot fully explain Robustness without coming back to KK. We started him as a struggling, impoverished child in Iran. Let's fast-forward to today and fill in some of the middle as we go. KK is seventy-five years of age. This is an important fact. Otherwise you would not believe what I am about to say, because most people would not consider it possible.*

At seventy-five, KK is likely more fit, more ripped, more buff, more pound-for-pound powerful than anyone you've ever met or seen. I used to train competition bodybuilders in college, and KK is right up there in sheer physique and strength with the best twenty-two-year-olds I ever trained.

Six days per week he does two-hour, nonstop, talk-to-nobody, super-intense, customized workouts that comprise Mixed Martial Arts (MMA) sparring with Ultimate Fighting Championship (UFC) world champions, and weights, in the toughest, no-nonsense, hard-core, Olympic-grade training

Khosro Khaloghli kickboxing at age fifty-nine.

gym in the region. I won't even mention the sets of 1,000-pound hack-slide squats he bangs out as just one small part of his routine. It's the same disciplined routine he's been doing for decades. Except, he looks tougher now.

He is frank about his condition: "Whenever I go into the gym, everyone knows I work the hardest." Although he might hesitate to brag, he is also the most fit. It's impossible to dispute, even when the next oldest guy in the gym is forty years younger.

Whether energy, inquisitiveness, joy, emotion, hope, focus, stamina, condition, or pure love of life—all the things that wear down so naturally in most human beings like the grit on used sandpaper—KK remains a stellar exemplar of what it means to be Robust, to maintain your ideal self, in spite of the hailstorm of all the unexpected stuff that life hurls your way. And as KK would tell you, the quality or nature of your GRIT has a huge effect on how Robust you can and will be. It would be easy to overlook that even someone like KK has dark moments—moments of doubt, sadness, hardship, and frustration—which will ultimately either erode or fortify you. Later in this book, you'll learn about the four GRIT Capacities—Emotional, Mental, Physical, and Spiritual—all of

Khosro Khaloghli, at age seventy-five, fresh from an invigorating workout on his estate.

which KK taps at different times to remain Robust, or recover his Robustness in even the most trying times. That's why looking at GRIT through a 3-D lens is so important.

• • • • • • • •

"Everybody wanna be a bodybuilder, but don't nobody wanna lift no heavy-ass weights!"
— RONNIE COLEMAN, EIGHT-TIME MR. OLYMPIA

GRIT 2.0—THE NEW PERSPECTIVE

You can Grok, Gauge, and Grow your GRIT along three axes or continua. The axes form the GRIT Grid Cube™, which is a three-dimensional way of visualizing how both the quality and quantity of GRIT come together into a high-octane mix, leading to Optimal GRIT.

THE GRIT GRID CUBE

Most people pick up a book called *GRIT* because they want more. That's a good start. But it's not enough. To go from Strong to Optimal, you want not just the most, but also the best possible GRIT. You want to gain ground on not just one, but all three axes as well. Quality can trump quantity. The GRIT Grid Cube puts these three axes together into one image and helps us view GRIT more holographically.

THE GRIT CONTINUA

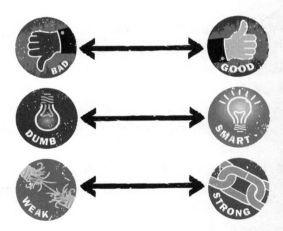

To understand the whole, we must understand the parts. That's why we'll explore each axis individually, starting with Bad-Good.

The truth is, there is Good GRIT and Bad. The difference may seem obvious. But the contrast can be disconcerting.

WARNING: Do not assume grit is a virtue.

BAD GRIT

The quickest way to discern if you are demonstrating Bad GRIT is to ask, "Does my pursuit of this goal have any unintended or intended negative consequence for me or others?" That's the key idea. People showing Bad GRIT relentlessly pursue goals that are ultimately damaging to themselves and/or others. It comes in three main forms that are worth exploring separately.

1. *Intentional Harm*—In some cases, they may deliberately seek to harm others.

2. *Me at Your Expense*—In other cases, they may simply strive to benefit themselves at others' cost.

3. *Unintentional*—Some of the most insidious cases of Bad GRIT arise when someone pursues an ultimately, even unforeseeably, damaging goal with the best of intentions.

Intentional Harm

While scanning the world for examples of the "Intentional Harm" version of Bad GRIT is not a particularly uplifting exercise, it's not terribly difficult to hit pay dirt. As my local deputy district attorney, Chase Martin, points out: "Read any crime report. It's a litany of people attempting and in many cases succeeding at harming and/or taking from others, in general to benefit themselves. That's why it's against the law. That's what makes it a crime." It can apply to some or all of G-R-I and T. Those making repeated, often creative attempts to commit the most damaging acts toward the most harmful goals, in spite of all the forces arrayed against them, are showing the most Bad GRIT.

GRIT Challenge—GRIT GONE BAD

I did not have to go find this story. It came to me. On May 23, 2014, a local man, Christopher Martinez, was gunned down by twenty-two-year-old mass murderer Elliot Rodger in Isla Vista, California. Beyond the horror Rodger unleashed by killing six people and injuring thirteen others before killing himself, was the deeply chilling relentlessness of his preparations. Apparently he worked tirelessly for years to save the $5,000 to purchase a Glock 34 pistol, which he then replaced with two SIG Sauer P226 pistols, deemed to be more accurate, to carry out his plan. He then methodically stockpiled ammunition. He wrote an extremely disturbing 107,000-word manifesto, titled "My Twisted World: The Story of Elliot Rodger." That's more than twice the length of this entire book. It seems he refined his plan countless times, to make sure he was successful in his final act. That's GRIT gone Bad.

Me at Your Expense

Bad GRIT goes beyond the obvious stuff, like crime, into the everyday behavior that can prove so disillusioning, demoralizing, and disappointing. This is where the "Me at Your Expense" version shows up. People who unrelentingly notch others down, minimize others to maximize themselves, take credit for others' good deeds, or steal other people's happiness to bolster their own, are showing more insidious forms of Bad GRIT.

People who tenaciously plot to sell you inferior products, where the price you pay far exceeds the value you enjoy, all to line their own pockets, are demonstrating Bad GRIT. People who persist in taking personal satisfaction from fueling your unhappiness are demonstrating a disturbing form of Bad GRIT. Bad GRIT comes in countless forms. I am sure you have been in its grip somewhere along the line. It's part of what challenges anyone's emotional Robustness, even faith.

KK *When KK and his team from Southern California came north to wrestle at California Polytechnic State University in San Luis Obispo, they had no money for hotels, so had to stay with local families. "I had an extra day, and the nice family who hosted me took me on a trip to Hearst Castle. I had never seen anything like it. I was overwhelmed by the beauty, by what this man [William Randolph] Hearst had built and accomplished," KK passionately explains.*

"So, I stood there, on that amazing patio, up on that mountain, overlooking the Pacific Ocean, and I say to myself, 'Someday Khosro have castle.'"

Roughly twenty years later, KK bought the most stunning piece of land, just up the road from Hearst Castle, to build his dream. Even KK could not have predicted the GRIT it would take to bring about his plan. The moment he filed a permit to build, he was told that what he was attempting to do was simply not possible. Not even close. So, for twenty years he battled and reasoned with the Coastal Commission, local councils, and any groups that opposed his efforts.

Today, KK and his wife, Haruka, enjoy one of the most spectacular properties in the world. They wanted to create something of unmatched beauty and quality, including exotic treasures from around the world to share with others. They invested a tremendous amount of money and effort to make it happen. And while they clearly achieved their goal, it was not without some give and take. One of the more obvious sacrifices was when KK was forced to remove a hundred fifty-foot-tall mature palm trees he had imported by ship from the Canary Islands. The Coastal Commission felt they violated the natural elements of the viewshed. KK lost millions of dollars, but is philosophical about what it took to achieve this portion of their dream. "It is not important to win. It is important everyone win, whenever possible."

KK makes it a point in any business deal he does, anywhere in the world, to have both sides walk away feeling as whole and good as possible. "People think you need to win," he explains, getting more adamant as he goes. "Let me ask you something. When you do that, who wins? I mean really? If you leave the other person damaged, no one wins. You have to help them keep their dignity, and go home feeling good about you and the deal you have together. I swim softly next to other people. I don't splash. I make sure we swim together."

A great example popped into the headlines this week. "Seat Reclining Rage" has ignited new battles in the sky over personal space. Three airline flights have been diverted just within eight days over apparent territorial meltdowns. In each case, passengers started heated arguments, disrupting their fellow travelers because, get this, someone pressed their button and, yes, reclined the seat. Airline travel can certainly demand a dose, and on some days a megadose, of GRIT. While everyone has to dig deep, do what it takes to endure what are typically less-than-ideal circumstances in order to get where they need to go, whether we do that in ways that inflict discomfort on others (Bad GRIT) or help ease the journey for others (Good GRIT) can literally determine everyone's ability to get there. This Bad vs. Good GRIT trade-off is about more than a given flight; it is about the human journey.

Unintentional

Bad GRIT is not just about someone being tenaciously evil; it's important to realize this—and a bit disturbing to point it out—because Bad GRIT can manifest as the third version. What was "good" but ultimately changed to "Unintentional Bad" is not just determined by one's initial aim. You have to also, most honestly, consider the outcome.

How often have you seen or heard someone with the best of intentions repeatedly say or do things that unintentionally hurt or damage others? I'd argue we are all guilty of such failings. I know I am. It just rips my heart out when I get super excited, put my best effort into something I'm convinced is extra thoughtful and magnanimous, only to have it turn out to be hurtful. Perhaps you've experienced something similar.

Anyone will tell you that one of the most potentially important but indisputably difficult, frustrating, expensive, and protracted odysseys in the world of collective human enterprise is bringing a new, life-enriching, or even lifesaving drug to market. It can take decades of relentless effort while facing a constant onslaught of adversity and slogging through the gauntlet of regulations, and of course spewing billions, even tens of billions of dollars.

I somehow doubt that Warner-Lambert Co. launched its revolutionary new diabetes drug, Rezulin, or Wyeth released Fen-Phen, to kill people. Even the release of the wonder painkiller-turned-mass-killer, Thalidomide, which malformed or killed more than 12,000 children worldwide, was hardly a terrorist act. Having worked with several of the top players in "Big Pharma," I am convinced that within their walls are some of the most talented people who are wholeheartedly dedicated to improving, as well as saving, human lives. I've seen them tear up over setbacks and delays, and weep profoundly when what they create actually and finally performs its intended miracles. Their intention could not be more pure. The result: collectively, thousands of deaths and tens of billions of dollars in ensuing lawsuits is the unintentional consequence.

"When you left the house today, you had the intention of putting clothes on and you did. You didn't try to put your pants on today. You simply put them on. The same has to hold for all of our intentions."

— PATCH ADAMS, MEDICAL DOCTOR, CLOWN, SOCIAL ACTIVIST

The world's charitable organizations save and enrich tens, if not hundreds of millions of lives each year. So, when largely impoverished Bangladesh faced an enormous health crisis, with more than a quarter-million children dying each year due to groundwater contamination, the charities stepped up in a big way to do the right thing.

They launched an immense humanitarian effort to bring cleaner water to Bangladeshis, installing roughly 10 million hand pumps to bring water from deep underground. The "good": it worked! But it ultimately changed to "Unintentional Bad"—and it took twenty years to realize this miraculous effort had backfired.

Yes, the water was free of the bacterial contaminations from surface sources. However, it was loaded with arsenic, the toxin that causes skin abrasions, cancer, and other diseases. Seventy-seven million people, or roughly half the population, were drinking water poisoned at levels beyond any acceptable standard. Studies have since shown a direct link with mortality rates. In short, what was intended as a massive gift became a mass poisoning of one of the world's more populous countries.

Look at genetically modified crops (GMOs). The intention of feeding a growing population is noble. If the link between GMOs and celiac disease, or gluten-related maladies now plaguing 18 million Americans proves true, the unintended consequence is far less noble.

This is why it takes both Good and Smart GRIT (see below) to effectively minimize and ideally eliminate Bad GRIT.

How many bosses, leaders, parents, teachers, and others in positions of authority have bruised people's egos, sapped their confidence, even left their followers and children devastated, all in the name of "tough love" or "constructive feedback"? And isn't it interesting to note that how well people respond to, and what they do with that feedback is largely determined by *their* GRIT? My goal, and I hope yours too, is to do whatever it takes to mitigate and eliminate Bad GRIT in any and all endeavors.

My **Bad** GRIT Example:

_____

_____

GOOD GRIT

People with Bad GRIT hurt others. People with Good GRIT do the opposite. One way to check, even amplify, your Good GRIT is to ask, "Is my pursuit of this goal intentionally or unintentionally benefiting others?"

Good GRIT often means doing something for yourself in a way that helps others. It's people like James Ward, the nineteen-year-old whose relentless effort to go from "Homeless to Howard" was more about benefiting his sister and brother than himself.

There is a reason the word "INTEGRITY" contains the word GRIT. It's tough to stick to and do what's right and good. People with Good GRIT strive for goals and objectives that prove to ultimately enrich or better others, and ideally themselves. But Good GRIT is rarely purely self-serving. Exercise is a good example. Although it may feed one's vanity, it also can dramatically improve the energy and quality-of-self one brings to others, while simultaneously reducing the potential burdens one puts on others. So, whether one exercises and gets fit for oneself or for others, done right, it tends to show Good GRIT, since everyone benefits from the effort and result.

GRIT Challenge—GOOD GRIT

Ronda Beaman is about the liveliest, most animated early baby boomer you could meet. No question, her superior fitness plays a huge role. She teaches barre exercise classes, boot camp, aerobics, spin, and is a personal fitness trainer for executives. That's her hobby. Professionally, "Dr. Ronda" has been a national award-winning professor, author, and international speaker, among her many accomplishments and pursuits. As a single then married and full-time employed mom, it took her eleven years to gut out her doctorate degree.

Her students adore her, and say, "Wherever her Climb may take her, she will leave a trail of smiles in her wake." When she puts her students through a fitness boot camp outside at 6:30 a.m. in the dead of winter, there's no question who the toughest, fittest person in the group happens to be.

Twenty-four years ago, she was also diagnosed with MS. Her doctor somberly explained that it was a progressive, degenerative disease, that some new medications might help slow or mitigate it a bit, but overall it was incurable. She was advised to reduce her stress, not push too hard, and try to enjoy whatever "good days" she could.

Twenty-four years later, she's never taken one pill, one shot, one dose of anything. In fact, she doesn't even talk about it. And if you saw her, you would realize that she shows no visible signs of her MS. Ronda explains why: "I used to work out to look good. I admit it! Now, I think of it as physical therapy. It's what allows me to take on life, every day."

Yes, she gets weird headaches sometimes. Yes, her shoulders occasionally scream with pain for no apparent reason. And no, heat is not her friend. But you would have no clue. She literally GRITs it out every day, living more fully than most people one-third her age. Oh, and I suppose I should tell you. She's also my wife. At times, she jokingly offers to switch roles, so I'm the one living this GRIT stuff while she writes the books!

Every time you put serious, protracted effort, especially personal sacrifice, into being loving, generous, kind, empathic, helpful, charitable, considerate, affirming, and selfless, you are demonstrating Good GRIT. The good news on Good GRIT is that its benefits tend to spread. Even when your effort is 100 percent focused on benefiting others, it almost always benefits you too.

GRIT Challenge—MORE GOOD GRIT

As I started asking around my community about best examples of Good GRIT, within my GRIT Challenge radius, I discovered that Catherine Ryan Hyde, best-selling author of the globally acclaimed book Pay It Forward, *happens to reside in the area. Turns out, the genesis of the idea came from the time her car broke down in a scary neighborhood at night, and two complete strangers helped her, then disappeared before she could thank them for saving her from a potentially dicey situation.* Pay It Forward, *the notion, book, and worldwide movement of anonymously doing good for others, spurring them to do the same, is a wonderful example of Good GRIT anyone can demonstrate, at any time.*

So, one simple way to show Good GRIT is to put your best effort into paying something positive forward to others, even when it's tough or inconvenient.

■ ■ ■ ■ ■ ■ ■ ■

Eric Schwartz is a local guy demonstrating some Good GRIT. Growing up in the smog-choked valleys of Los Angeles, he decided it'd be a good idea to start a company that customized bikes to people who don't typically ride, as a way to get them more comfortable with this mode of healthful transportation. His start-up, Commuter Bikes, is as much a cause as a business that provides real benefits to the entire community. It's tough to launch a successful bicycle company in an already packed market. But as Eric explains, "We are dedicated to bicycle advocacy and, as our name suggests, utility bicycles. We do not feature mountain bikes, and we sell few racing bikes. We focus on effective, all-weather, transportation cycles." By selling more-accessible, less-intimidating bikes to the nontraditional rider, Eric gets more people arriving at work and school with greater health and vitality, causing no ecological downside, by being self-propelled. His GRIT does good.

People who demonstrate Good GRIT tend to be more respected, trusted, admired, appreciated, sought after, befriended, included, and loved. They tend to be happier and healthier. They even live longer.

KK *As robust as he is, KK was slammed to the mat when he came back from one of his many overseas business trips last year suffering from some mysterious, exotic bug. It became so serious that he lost forty-five pounds and was told he might not recover. He might die. He and his wife had to quietly confront the real possibilities.*

Ten doctors worked his case, at the finest hospitals. His stubborn GRIT surely paid off. "I just got up and left. I had to leave the hospital to get better." His doctor, recently explained: "About one-third of people with this mysterious condition die. One-third never recover. And one-third survive. But no one comes out like KK did. He has more muscle mass; he is bigger and stronger than he was before he got sick. And at his age? Amazing."

I asked KK, if he had died, what he would like to be remembered for. How he would like to be described by those who knew him best. Given that today he is a global titan, CEO of companies across a mind-bendingly diverse assortment of industries, you might guess he would want to be remembered for his accomplishments, his wealth, or his materially apparent immense success. Instead, he paused, leaned forward, looked at me with blazing, unblinking eyes, and said softly, slowly, and surely, "He was a gentle man. He was a kind man. He was a good man. You see, that to me is success."

There are some stories you hear (or read) that seem faked or contrived. They fall so far outside the bell curve that our first impulse is to dismiss them with a simple, "As if!" or "No way." This is one such story, which I have, for my needs and yours, verified from multiple sources. And I hope you can absorb it for its genuine purpose. I had to ask permission from KK, and be a bit persuasive, to share with you something no one else knows. As I mentioned, he is a humble man, and the only reason he agreed to let me share this is (as I pointed out to him) in hopes that it will inspire you, as it has his wonderful wife, Haruka, and as it has me.

Every day KK loads his pockets with cash and whenever he sees a person in need, he stops and gives them whatever he has. Every—and yes, he insists, every—hitchhiker, no matter what location or time of day, he picks them up. If he has to stop traffic to help someone, he does. Sometimes, he intentionally drives to the toughest places, where he knows he can help. During the darkest hours of Christmas Eve, he can be found driving by needle-using addicts and prostitutes under a railroad bridge in the worst neighborhood of LA. If that's what it takes to bring these people some cheer and help, he goes.

"It can be $5,000, $200, or $20, I don't know, and I don't care. It is not mine. No! It is theirs, you see? I don't care if I miss my flight. I don't care if I miss my meeting. I don't care if it is day or night, in even the most dangerous neighborhood. It does not matter. No one hurts me. I am a tough neighborhood! If I have to drive 200 miles out of my way to take someone somewhere, I take them. Now."

His gratitude and good fortune compel him. "I am so lucky. Who am I to drive in a beautiful car with full stomach and air conditioning on, and here is this guy nobody will pick up. Is he hungry? Whenever I am traveling, I see old people and try to help them. Sometimes, I just sit and talk to them, because nobody does that. It is my job; it is my honor to help. Every time. Every person. Every day. To do these things, this is the most important thing I do. Nothing else compares."

· · · · · · · ·

GRIT is like cholesterol. It's not about your pure amount. It's about the combined amount, the actual proportion or ratio of good vs. bad cholesterol you have. Increasing your Good offsets a certain amount of Bad. The same applies to GRIT.

People with Good GRIT tend to become leaders, because most people are drawn to and are more prone to follow the direction and vision of someone with Good GRIT. KK has people literally lined up to do deals with him and to work with him. It's authentic, and people see that.

The gravitational pull of Good GRIT is powerful. That's why savvy leaders, including those running for political office, tend to intentionally highlight their Good GRIT values and efforts, as well as any successful track record. While GRIT is not inherently a virtue, Good GRIT comes a lot closer to earning such revered status, especially when you add the one missing element: avoiding Dumb GRIT.

My **Good** GRIT Example:

_____

_____

死馬當活馬醫

Chinese Proverb

Translation: *Try to save the dead horse as if it is still alive.*
Meaning: *Do the impossible, for it may truly be possible.*

DUMB GRIT

Ever hear someone, maybe someone you respect, nobly proclaim, with eyes ablaze as he or she dives back into the fray, "I *never* quit!" As impressive as that may sound, it may also be somewhat limiting, if not insanely stupid. One way to check if you're demonstrating Dumb GRIT is to ask, "In what ways is this goal, or the way I am going after this goal, less intelligent than it could otherwise be?" Then listen to the answer!

The fact is, the world is filled with both Dumb GRIT and Smart GRIT. Dumb GRIT is basically some combination of pursuing "less than ideal" goals with "less than ideal" strategies. In some instances, it frankly can boil down to going after really dumb stuff in really dumb ways. At minimum, Dumb GRIT slows you down. More often than not, it ups the toll you pay for your efforts. It can also cause you to fail. Ultimately, it can lead to tragedy. When it becomes damaging, Dumb GRIT ends up morphing into Dumb-Bad GRIT. This happens when you end up hurting people by relentlessly pursuing the wrong stuff in the wrong ways.

A good friend of mine in college had her mind set on getting into law school. Her father, whom she pretty much worshipped, was a prominent attorney in LA. Although he never seemed to have time to be with her, she held this hero syndrome close to her heart. She was extremely bright and doggedly persistent.

She decided, probably due to her father's sagas of hardship, that she had to martyr herself to the cause of becoming a lawyer like dad. She knew her solid grades would not be enough. So, she all but killed herself studying for the LSAT (Law School Admission Test) late into the night, after grueling days at work, month after month. She became a hermit, refusing anyone's help or any outside tutoring. The transformation was heartbreaking. She became lethargic, lost her spark and stamina, and worst of all, failed the test.

She decided to redouble her efforts and try again. The second time around, she barely slept, ate junk food, blew off any remaining relationships, and sequestered herself nearly 24/7 in her quest to pass the exam. She failed again

She repeated, but intensified the same strategy and effort not twice, but *three* times. And each time, the damage got successively more severe. She certainly had Strong but tragically Dumb GRIT.

Dumb GRIT occurs when a person either:

A) Continues to relentlessly go after something or some version of something that is no longer worth achieving or pursuing and/or

B) Repeatedly uses the same approach or an array of ineffective, or at least less-than-optimal, strategies to achieve that goal.

Concordia University psychologist Carsten Wrosch investigates the nuances of giving up. "The notion of persistence is deeply embedded within the American culture," he comments, along with his coauthor, Gregory Miller, in their article in the journal *Psychological Science*. They and dozens of studies argue that there are times when it is psychologically beneficial to give up rather than persist. In a particularly poignant study, Wrosch, and his colleagues Jutta Heckhausen and William Fleeson, discovered that among women who were highly motivated but biologically unable to have children through natural or medical means, most gave up after the age of forty. Those who persisted in trying, when all the evidence indicated otherwise, were the most depressed.

This process of goal disengagement can be beneficial. Assuming there are only so many hours in the day and one's life, working toward things that have some chance of success vs. genuine impossibilities makes sense. This doesn't mean giving up on the tough stuff, or taking on lower standards. It does mean exercising Smart vs. Dumb GRIT, and going after the best version of the most important goals, in the most effective and promising ways.

As with Bad GRIT, we're *all* guilty of Dumb GRIT. It's a matter of frequency and degree. If you have only experienced extremely rare instances demonstrating extremely mild doses of Dumb GRIT, consider yourself lucky and, well, *smart*. Most people don't recognize their own Dumb GRIT in action. Dumb GRIT rarely feels dumb. In fact, it tends to feel noble, which is why our GRIT can get dumber before we get smarter. I hope that with this awareness and the tools provided in this book, you can get there sooner, with more upside and briefer, shallower downsides.

I'll never forget Bob Atkinson for as long as I live. He was arguably the most relentless salesman I've ever met. Great guy too. Unfortunately, he was also one of the tragically least effective. And it wasn't because he wasn't doing his job exactly as he was instructed to do it.

"The only thing that I see that is distinctly different about me is I'm not afraid to die on a treadmill. I will not be outworked, period. You might have more talent than me, you might be smarter than me, you might be sexier than me, you might be all of those things — you got it on me in nine categories. But if we get on the treadmill together, there're two things: You're getting off first, or I'm going to die. It's really that simple ..."

— WILL SMITH, OSCAR-NOMINATED ACTOR AND GRAMMY AWARD-WINNING MUSICIAN

He was selling long-distance dial-up service to business customers for one of the early competitors of AT&T, when "Ma Bell" broke up. No one worked harder than Bob. He was the first one on the phones in the morning, made more than one hundred calls to frigid leads, cold-calling, or "dialin' and smilin'" as he called it, from dawn to long past dusk. The more dismal his sales, the longer and harder he worked.

The problem was, every cold call was exactly the same. And every follow-up call was exactly the same.

"Hello, Ms. Johnson, this is Bob with North American Telephone. How are you on this fine day?"

"Good, good. Well, I know how busy you must be, and I wouldn't want to disturb you unless I had something really important to tell you. I've been analyzing the numbers, and did you know your long-distance phone bill is 40 percent higher than it should be?"

"I understand why you're shocked. I was too! That's why I felt I had to call you right away to alert you to the situation. The good news is, I believe I can help you."

"You're welcome, you're welcome. The only inconvenience is, I need you to do three simple things: 1) I need you to sign something that says you're going to shift to this upgraded service. 2) I'm going to have to send my technician to your house to install a small device on your phone line; he'll be there sometime between 8 a.m. and 5 p.m. on Tuesday. And, oh, 3) he'll be collecting a check for $250 from you, just a onetime charge to cover the switch to the upgraded service."

"Oh, I see ... yes, I understand. Well, that's no problem at all, I'll simply call you back at the end of the month and give you another chance to take me up on this special upgrade offer."

"Oh, you don't." Then in one quick breath and burst, "Well that's entirely OK, it's no inconvenience at all, I'll just call you in a couple weeks, thank you, Ms. Johnson," followed by an urgent click, Bob's deep sigh, a pause, then the sound of him picking up the phone to do it again, and again, and again …

Two weeks later: "Hello, Ms. Johnson, it's Bob again with North American Telephone, calling, as promised, to give you another chance to save 40 percent off your phone bill …"

"Hello, Ms. Johnson? Hello?"

Bob's problem was, he was given a script, and unlike some of his coworkers who altered the script, even the entire approach, in order to achieve success in a more palatable way, Bob stuck to the script. When his attempts failed, he stuck to it even harder. And if he got rejected, he called back sometimes seven to ten times, per customer, resulting in countless complaints against the company.

The trick is—unlike Bob, and more like his more successful coworkers—to learn to spot and correct your moments of Dumb GRIT, before others do! And the best way to do that is to exercise a higher proportion and degree of Smart GRIT.

> *"If at first you don't succeed try, try again. Then quit.*
> *There's no point in being a damn fool about it."*
> — W. C. FIELDS, COMEDIAN AND ACTOR

My Dumb GRIT Example:

_____

_____

SMART GRIT

Smart GRIT shines forth when you have the courage and clarity to:

A) Step back at the right moments to ask, "Is this goal still worth pursuing?" and "If so, why?" then,

B) Adjust your approach/strategy appropriately and agilely to at least increase your chances of fulfilling that goal. Smart GRIT means knowing when to quit. Smart GRIT means giving your above-and-beyond best to the right things, in the right ways, for the right reasons.

"The trouble with most people is they think with their hopes or fears or wishes rather than with their minds."
— **WILL DURANT, PHILOSOPHER, AUTHOR OF** *THE STORY OF PHILOSOPHY*

In my first book, *Adversity Quotient*, I equated your life aspiration with a mountain. Physical mountains inspire us. Our personal mountains compel us. Over the decades, I've discovered that people seem to share a core human drive to ascend, to move forward and up along one's mountain or purpose in one's life. But it's tough. If defining—let alone staying true to a worthy aspiration for one's life—were easy, more people would make it happen. The vast majority stop short or bail out.

My PEAK Team and I break down people's response to the challenges of life into three broad categories: Quitters, Campers, and Climbers. Quitters throw in the towel; they give up on the tougher and potentially most "gritifying" pursuits in life. Campers make up the vast majority of any workforce, and perhaps humankind. Our global data suggests, 80 percent of people fall into this category.

Campers reach a point where they essentially say "enough" or "good enough," and they settle in. They set up camp. Their energy then goes largely into campground preservation, which can make them change- and risk-averse, as well as in a state of gradual atrophy. What originally was a motivation of relief from the arduous ascent and conditions becomes a motivation of fear, fear of anything that messes with or threatens the campground.

Only the Climbers continue to learn, grow, strive, and evolve. Only the Climbers stay fully alive until their final breath. Only the Climbers sustain the GRIT to create and enjoy an Optimal Life.

I've asked more than 1 million people around the world what percentage of those attending their 25-year high school reunion have successfully stayed true to a defining, worthy purpose in their lives. Every group responds, 10 percent or less. That's why I spend some time trying to decode why and how some people Quit, most people Camp, and the rare GRITty elite Climb. They move forward and up along that adversity-strewn terrain, through the most harrowing conditions, regardless of the difficulties and struggles involved.

Here's the problem. It's not enough to be a Climber at your work or in general life. I've also discovered plenty of Climbers with Dumb Grit who pound their heads to a bloody pulp, smacking those noggins over and over against the same impenetrable overhang, failing to discover that rocks apparently make poor sparring partners for skulls. They fail to understand that W. E. Hickson's centuries-old advice, "If at first you don't succeed try, try, try again," should be amended: "If after repeated, heartfelt attempts you don't make any progress, step back to reassess and refine your goal and/or your strategy for achieving it, to at least increase your chances of success."

Climbers with Smart Grit understand the difference. They know when to step back, reassess, and just as importantly, reroute. Conditions change. Assumptions get shattered. Uncertainty is definite. Demonstrating Smart or agile GRIT is the only way to continue your ascent.

KK *When KK was showing some Chinese dignitaries around the wine country of the Central Coast of California, they immediately decided to form a joint venture, bringing California wine to China. Apparently the Chinese appetite for premium wine is currently pretty boundless.*

Using his Growth mindset, KK researched every possible grape grower and wine producer. His initial goal was to partner with one of the biggest, most prestigious brands to produce a premium wine. But after his initial investigation, KK decided to reroute and take a different path.

He asked around and explored the most important factors, like transportation to a harbor via freeways and the capacity to produce an unlimited volume. He then pursued the winery that fit those criteria, knowing he would have to upgrade almost everything to make it work.

"The goal is set," he explains, in his typical warm but intense, teacher mode. "That is not in question. But you have to be flexible. You must be agile in how you pursue that goal. Four years ago, what did I know about wine? Nothing! Now we have one of the most successful wine businesses in the United States. And we will sell it for a very handsome profit ... Being open to change how you get your goal. This is the thing."

Sometimes it's easier to estimate how Smart or Dumb GRIT is by looking at the results rather than the path. That's the satisfying part of the challenge—having your GRIT end up Smart. I love Robert Redford's explanation of how his little mountain paradise, Sundance Resort, came to be:

The first year, I couldn't get a loan from the bank. The waiters didn't show up, so the owners had to wait on tables. The stable master was more interested in the female customers than in the horses, and the horses from our stables wandered in confusion all over the canyon. The Sundance Summer Festival was launched with a misfired rocket that lay fizzling on the stage. Vehicles stalled, sewers backed up, we were robbed, and the tree in the Tree Room died. A potential early investor who spoke eloquently about his belief in our concept was hauled away by men in white suits. But we endured.

To *endure*. To persevere through the insanity, frustration, struggle, and sacrifice. This is what GRIT is all about. Doing it *smarter* is what makes it both more enjoyable and more likely to succeed. How often does a goal lose its luster, when a modified version of that goal, or at least the path to get there, might be smarter and better than the initial one? Exercising Smart GRIT can be fun!

GRIT Challenge — SMART GRIT

Sometimes Smart GRIT can show up in the most endearing or, in this case, a somewhat conniving way. Down the street lives the nicest couple you could hope to meet, Rod and Lorrie Curb. As I explained Smart GRIT to them, they looked at each other, laughed, and good-naturedly shared this humorous tale of their version of Smart GRIT from their recent European adventures.

"We were at Leeds Castle in Kent and decided to take on their famous challenge: the maze and grotto. The maze is immense, an impenetrable six-foot-plus-high thicket made of 2,400 yew trees.

"I was busy enjoying some ice cream with family and friends," Rod explained. "So Lorrie, being a bit competitive, took off for the maze and dared me to catch up with her. Well, the moment I got there and saw the immensity of the challenge, I realized this could take a while, to say the least. I'd heard people sometimes spend hours running into dead ends and getting lost. So, rather than diving in and getting lost, I scanned the situation and spotted the official docent perfectly perched up high in the center of the maze. I watched him for a while and waited for him to catch my eye. We looked at each other, and then he appeared to almost wink. It would have been so easy to miss. But with the absolute slightest and almost indiscernible nod of his head, he seemed to be suggesting an initial direction.

"So, rather than question, I dove in. Each time I got stuck, I waited for his gaze. Anyone else watching him would never even notice his expertly covert guidance. A twitch to the left, a wink to the right, a glance down the center, and on it went, until my stunned and amazed wife found the docent and me waving across the maze at her. She'd been trying to solve it, bumping against dead ends for forty-five minutes, sweaty, huffy, thirsty, while I was standing there finished, in the shade, and enjoying the view. Let it never be said again that men can't ask for directions!"

• • • • • • • • •

My **Smart** GRIT Example:
_____
_____

WEAK GRIT

It's humbling when you ask yourself, "Am I digging as deep, doing as much, and enduring all I can to make it happen?" If your answer falls short, you may be demonstrating Weak, or at least weaker than ideal, GRIT.

Weak GRIT in no way implies an inability to set meaningful goals, with elevating intentions and powerful potential. Weak GRIT is simply a limited or lack of capacity to do what it takes to make it happen—especially in the face of frustrations, difficulties, setbacks, and delays, and especially as the path to making it happen requires greater effort and more time.

Those with Weak GRIT can become notorious for both setting goals and making compelling promises that remain chronically unfulfilled. In that way, Weak GRIT can pose a challenge to one's integrity and trustworthiness, especially when it comes to the tough stuff. The quantity—the strength or degree—of one's GRIT can at times trump the quality. This is why so many employers today look for GRIT over any other quality. Even a combination of Smart and Good, when mixed with Weak GRIT, has limited if any real potential. Weak GRIT also implies a fairly anemic showing on most, if not all, dimensions of GRIT.

My **Weak** GRIT Example:

_____

_____

STRONG GRIT

If you can answer a resounding "Yes!" to the question, "Am I digging as deep, doing as much, and enduring all I can to make it happen?" that's Strong GRIT. Strong GRIT is the inverse of Weak GRIT. It implies an exceptional capacity to dig deep, do whatever it takes—even sacrifice, struggle, and suffer—to get things done. Those with Strong GRIT are often trusted, sought-after friends and team members for tackling and successfully achieving difficult goals. But that only holds true if one's GRIT is also sufficiently Good and Smart.

Strong is not enough. If one has Strong but Dumb and/or Bad GRIT, that simply implies it will be dumber and "badder" as a result. Adding more fuel, going faster and harder in the wrong direction, is not an ideal tendency.

GRIT Challenge—STRONG, BAD, and DUMB GRIT

A dear friend of mine had a father who loved her, but who was inherently a mean-spirited guy. Whenever he disliked one of her friends, which was his automatic norm, he would do whatever it took to eliminate that friend from his daughter's life. One time, he humiliated not only the friend, but also the friend's entire family, while spewing various racial epithets, just to seal the termination. Although it was not at all atypical, when it drove her to tears of desperation and mortification, he simply told her he was doing what was best for her.

On top of that, he had a long history of making terrible, often tragic decisions. Despite being offered advice to the contrary, he moved his family dozens of times, taking on new jobs, losing money almost every time, and putting them deeper and deeper in debt. He decided his wife should not be allowed to take classes, jobs, or even learn to drive. Not the best decisions. But he had one consistent trait. He always stuck to his guns, and he never backed down. No debate. No remorse. Strong, Bad, and Dumb GRIT make a scary combination, resulting in some of the scariest characters you can imagine or ever meet. The inverse, and the pathway to avoid these GRIT-related downsides, is the aspirational ideal—Optimal GRIT.

My **Strong** GRIT Example:

_____

_____

OPTIMAL GRIT

Optimal GRIT is the brass ring. It is what we all should reach for in all we do. Optimal GRIT is nothing less than the ideal combination of quantity and quality. That's why this is the central intention of the final—**Grow-Advanced**—section of this book.

⬡ Optimal GRIT: When you consistently and reliably demonstrate your fullest, "goodest," smartest, and strongest GRIT to achieve your most worthy goals.

To test the power of this concept, ask yourself this question that I've been asking groups around the world for years: Who is the single greatest human being? Living or dead, famous or unknown, whom do you pick? Try to vividly picture that person, right now. Without even knowing whom you chose, I would predict two things. First, the person you picked showed the closest you've seen to Optimal GRIT. Second, I'd predict that had your pick not demonstrated something close to Optimal GRIT, you never would have chosen that person.

The symbiotic bond between greatness and GRIT also holds when you flip the equation. Ask yourself, given what you now know, who is the greatest exemplar (living or dead, known or unknown) of not just grit, but also Optimal (high, good, smart) GRIT? Start there. As you imagine that person, on a scale of 1–10, how does he or she rate on overall or relative greatness? Chances are you arrive at the same answers.

OK, so now you get it. Chances are you "Grok" the basics of GRIT (G-R-I-T, Smart vs. Dumb, Good vs. Bad, Strong vs. Weak) plenty well enough to go on to the basics of how to Gauge yours. Nearly a million people worldwide have gained fresh, vital insights from our (PEAK's) assessments. I trust you too will enjoy the rich benefits and perspective the GRIT Gauge can provide, as your next step.

GAUGE

THE BASICS

Now you're ready to gauge your GRIT using the **GRIT Gauge™— the world's preeminent assessment of GRIT.** My intent is to help you establish the starting point from which you grow, evolve, and ideally reassess your progress on GRIT in the weeks, months, and years ahead. The GRIT Gauge will also provide the perfect foundation for you to go on and complete the GRIT Mix as you move up to the Advanced Level.

TAKE THE **GRIT GAUGE**™

With your purchase of this book, you receive a free personal unique ID to click and complete the online GRIT Gauge™. It will require roughly five minutes to complete and will provide you with a comprehensive report, including scores, descriptions, graphs, and tips to help you understand where you are now, and to even begin some initial steps for growing your GRIT.

This is the same robust, proven tool used at top universities and companies worldwide.

Before proceeding,
complete the GRIT Gauge now
at **www.gritgauge.com**

You already know how much and why GRIT matters. You also know, based on our work with hundreds of thousands of people worldwide spanning three decades, GRIT is something that can be permanently, measurably improved. The missing step is to get a clear understanding of where you are now. So let's dig in.

I hope you've spent some time really marinating in the feedback you received with your GRIT Gauge Feedback Report. There's little point in my drilling deeper into your specific numbers. Rather my intention is not to repeat, but to go beyond and help you extract even more out of your results. I thought you might want to know some hidden truths about GRIT.

GRIT Composite Score

The most important thing to remember is your score is not a tattoo. It's merely an indicator of where you are now relative to the massive database of people like you, worldwide, who've assessed their GRIT. It's your starting point, from which you grow and improve.

It's also important to point out that "Average" isn't average. The GRIT Gauge bell curve is artificially inflated purely because we've assessed people like you— people who want to learn and improve. You're part of a special group that already scores higher than the general population overall. If the database were more representative of the entire population, we know for a fact that the means and cutoffs for each range would drop substantially. All your GRIT score tells you is how you stack up against others sort of like you.

What your results *don't* tell you is that your GRIT composite score (the big number) is arguably as important, and sometimes less important than your G,R,I,T individual numbers. Here's why. The more level or even your G,R,I,T scores/graph appears, the less the individual scores reveal, and the more meaning your composite GRIT score tends to have. But if you are like most people who have some noticeable differences among your G,R,I,T scores, those may actually reveal the richer ore when it comes to insights and what you may wish to focus on growing, going forward.

It's also important to point out that the GRIT Gauge is distinct from the various style-or personality-related surveys you may be familiar with or have experienced in the past. Those tend to be "descriptive," meaning they simply describe your various (usually) behavioral tendencies, strengths, fears, weaknesses, etc. The idea is, no one type, personality, profile, or category is superior to another. They're just different. And I hope that in the process of understanding yourself and others, you can avoid some unnecessary relational crud by appreciating and interacting with everyone more effectively.

The GRIT Gauge is "normative." This simply means, unlike those other assessments, in this case, overall higher is pretty much better. In case you're wondering, KK scores in the top 1 percent of the world on overall GRIT. That's why, for people like him—and for you, as your overall GRIT improves—it becomes the defining element that shapes and propels one's narrative. "Normative" means it's better for you, better for the people you influence, hang with, lead, partner with, team up with, and for anyone who counts on you for anything. The higher your GRIT (as long as it's Good and Smart), the more upsides and potentially fewer downsides.

Growth

The hidden headline about Growth is, the more intense life gets, the harder this one is to do, let alone really optimize. If a big chunk of Growth is the degree to which you seek and consider fresh angles, approaches, perspectives, and information as you adjust and fortify your pursuit of your goals, letting that dwindle can be highly limiting, if not perilous.

GRIT Challenge—GROWTH

As part of my GRIT Challenge, I stopped off at a coffee shop in my little town, just as some well-heeled tourist in black leathers and black helmet zoomed up on his gorgeous, new, red, fully loaded Ducati motorcycle, striking a sharp contrast with the low-key, bicycle-riding locals.

"Hey, nice bike!" I offered, as he headed in for an espresso.

He paused, turned, smiled, and sighed, "Yeah. Thanks. To be honest, I'm still learning how to ride that rocket."

"How fast are we talking?"

"Well, I shouldn't admit this, but, I had that thing up to 185!" he confessed, looking around conspiratorially.

"Wow! Amazing. Really, what was that like?"

He put his hands out in front of him about three feet apart, and suddenly brought them to about six inches apart. "That's exactly what the road does. It's tunnel vision. And it's intense. You can't see anything but this suddenly super-thin strip in front of you. It's pretty freaky. I never experienced anything like it before."

• • • • • • •

That's how life works. The faster and harder you go, the narrower your focus naturally becomes. We get increasingly intent on just doing or pursuing that thing, in that way, because that's all we have time to consider, let alone accomplish. The irony is, unless we're really deliberate, in the moments when we need to demonstrate Growth-related behaviors the most is when we access and show them the least.

This means the higher you score on Growth, the more naturally you demonstrate these behaviors. But your score does not guarantee consistency over time and across situations. Regardless of your number, the more consistently and completely you can keep your mind open to and actively seeking the most useful alternatives, the stronger *and smarter* your GRIT becomes.

Resilience

Here's the hidden story on this factor. There's no question that, as the world has gotten a little more wacky, challenging, uncertain, and complex, resilience has risen to premier status among what it takes to thrive in today's times. But as the guy who's written four books on the subject, I've got to tell you, resilience is essential, but it's not enough. In fact, I've found in some cases highly resilient people remain strong and vibrant, but they just don't make any progress. It's almost as if they get so juiced by handling adversity that they lose sight of the end goal.

I remember one time I was climbing with Dan, a pretty go-for-it guy, in the back rock canyons of Santa Barbara. We set off to get to the top, enjoy the views, and make our way down by sunset. I was following his lead, since we were in his backyard. A short ways in, we ended up in a somewhat bad place. He wanted to show off one of his favorite spots, which apparently had stunning waterfalls in the wet season. To get there, we had to free-climb up a series of sheer, fairly smoothed-out, increasingly tall, slick rock faces. I'm not ashamed to admit, as we got higher and higher, it got scarier and scarier. It became clear that one slip and it could be game over. And because of our original plan, we didn't even have helmets. I couldn't help but wonder if this was the best route.

It also became clear that the more difficult it became, the more pumped Dan was getting. He was in his element! Dan was clearly getting stoked by the danger, and was drawn by the thrill of going deeper and higher. As you might guess, we never made it to the top. We spent our whole time trying to find a safe way down and out of this unexpected diversion. Thriving on adversity doesn't mean you accomplish your goals.

Whatever your score, it's not just how much of it you have, but also how well you use what you have to accomplish what you set out to do. As your Resilience gets stronger, you'll want to also strive to use it well, for the right challenges and setbacks, and employing it in ways that create the greatest potential progress toward your goals.

Instinct

The degree to which you step back, reassess, and potentially reroute/readjust both your pursuits and your path is obviously a huge component of not just GRIT; it is particularly important to Smart GRIT as well. In fact, of the four dimensions, Instinct is arguably, or at least potentially, the single most potent contributor in shifting from less Dumb to more Smart GRIT. This can save you a lot of hurt and gain you a whole lot of fresh ground.

KK *That's part of what not just keeps our friend KK in the game, but also puts him at the top of his game, at an age when others are well past their prime. He drives home the point as he leans in, with his signature smile, confiding, "Paul, when it comes to being agile, as you say, I have an unfair advantage! When I am in that room, with those people, doing that deal, I look around. I ask myself, how many buildings have these people done? How many failures, lessons, committees, permits, banks, and headaches have they had to navigate? Because I have done this the longest, in many cases I have learned the most, so I can adjust more effectively, more quickly. You see?"*

• •• • • • • ••

While experience matters, it is not required to grow your Instinct. In the next section of the book, **GROW,** you will learn tools you can apply now to improve your Instinct. Wherever you score now, you can probably imagine how deeply you will benefit as your Instinct grows, helping you spend more time and energy on the path toward what matters most.

Tenacity

Although on GRIT overall, more is better, when it comes to Tenacity, that is not always the case. Tenacious how? For what? In what ways? These are the often humbling questions we have to ask.

GRIT Challenge—TENACITY GONE BAD

As part of my GRIT Challenge, I reached out to a distant neighbor whom I did not know that well. I did know his reputation as a brutally effective, do-whatever-it-takes-to-win attorney. I was told he was the kind of guy who would eat his young to win a case. In all fairness, he was and is as nice as can be to me.

But when he shared the story and facts around one of his many victorious cases, I really had to wonder if the pain and hardship he caused to certain people, in order to win damages for others, was worth it, or if it had a positive result. He finished the story, "So people know I win. And you know why? Because I just don't give up. I find a way. They count on me for that. I do whatever it takes."

So if Instinct can contribute the most to having smarter GRIT, Tenacity-gone-bad can be the single biggest feeder of Dumb GRIT, the kind that even unintentionally causes harm to you and/or others. What's the moral? Especially as your Tenacity grows, be sure to be funneling it into the right things in the least damaging and most ultimately beneficial ways.

Sample GRIT Profiles

While explicating all the implications of every possible combination of G, R, I, and T would consume its own (immensely boring!) book, you may gain some potent insights from one of the following common examples.

The Pained Pioneer	GROWTH	RESILIENCE	INSTINCT	TENACITY
HIGH	●		●	
AVERAGE				
LOW		●		●

People with this sort of profile tend to step back, reassess, seek new ideas and angles, even reroute as necessary to keep going, but usually at a significant cost. This is what happens when someone has exceptionally Smart, but only modest overall GRIT.

Almost any path is riddled with adversity. For a person with this profile, progress comes at a price, one they may, over time, decide is no longer worth paying. Why? Because they may lack the resilience to remain tenacious in the face of the daily onslaught—the setbacks, challenges, obstacles, disappointments, uncertainties, failures, problems, difficulties, glitches, and implosions—that can randomly but predictably challenge anyone's GRIT and progress.

The Bloody Stump

	GROWTH	RESILIENCE	INSTINCT	TENACITY
HIGH		●		●
AVERAGE				
LOW	●		●	

If you haven't lived this, you've seen it. This is the person who tends to never quit, who is undaunted in the face of adversity, and refuses to consider alternate angles, reassess, or reroute, even when it's advisable and appropriate.

One of the most humorous examples of a bloody stump profile comes from the 1975 classic *Monty Python and the Holy Grail*, where the Black Knight confronts King Arthur.

Here's an abbreviated version:

Hailstorm Hero

	GROWTH	RESILIENCE	INSTINCT	TENACITY
HIGH	●		●	●
AVERAGE				
LOW		●		

People with this profile have almost the full package, but lack one vital ingredient: Resilience. Relentlessly (T) going after the right goals in the best ways (I), and seeking alternative approaches, insights, and strategies along the way (G), is a powerful but incomplete combination. Adversity will take a significant, accumulated toll. The pummeling brought on by the slings and arrows of life may cause more than mere dings and dents. While this person might make it through the storm and arrive at the summit, the storm gear may need replacing.

The Sufficer

	GROWTH	RESILIENCE	INSTINCT	TENACITY
HIGH				
AVERAGE	●	●	●	●
LOW				

This profile is fairly common. It shows a modest or average level of GRIT, across the board. No one dimension stands out, up or down. The result is, this person usually has and does just enough. Just enough to keep going, eventually get there, on enough things, to have a decent life and reasonable career, and be able to look back and say, "I did OK." Or, "Not all bad." If you find this description uninspiring, that's intentional and authentic. People with this profile tend to develop a limited appetite for audacious goals, especially when the path is clearly dominated by rough, unpredictable conditions and terrain. By definition, a person with this profile is unlikely to fulfill, let alone relentlessly expand or exploit, his or her potential. An overall upgrade of one's GRIT is in order.

All of these profiles, and certainly your G-R-I-T Profile, can come more fully to light when held against the backdrop of Robustness. The wear-and-tear factor, for some, can be even more important than GRIT itself.

Robustness

This factor and score are a rough answer to the question, "GRIT, at what price?" Yes, it's common for overall GRIT and overall Robustness to correlate, or walk in stride. Higher GRIT tends toward greater Robustness. And the inverse is also true. But there are plenty of exceptions.

GRIT at a Price

	GROWTH	RESILIENCE	INSTINCT	TENACITY	ROBUSTNESS
HIGH	●	●	●	●	
AVERAGE					
LOW					●

It's important to dig deeper on Robustness, which comprises two main parts: Life Lens and Accumulated Effect, how tough you consider your life to have been and how positively or negatively it has affected you so far. The interplay between these two elements is as important as your overall Robustness score.

If, for example, you feel you've faced moderate or less adversity, but score worse than most on the wear and tear, that implies a vulnerability to the accumulated challenges and disappointments yet to come. If, however, your life has been particularly adversity-rich, but the Accumulated Effect is purely positive, as is exactly the case with KK's GRIT Gauge scores, then in our vernacular, we would say you clearly have a pattern of not enduring, or even overcoming, but truly *harnessing* adversity. Your GRIT makes you more robust. And you are grateful for your adversity. You wouldn't trade it for anything!

What I've discovered over and over in my research is that it is entirely possible for someone to score relatively high on overall GRIT, but modest to low on Robustness. This means that, like cheap sandpaper, they may wear down more easily and quickly, in comparison to their more Robust counterparts. For the high-GRIT/low-Robustness people, GRIT may have a dark side, fueling them to relentlessly pursue things that actually accelerate their wear and tear. Conversely, you could have moderately low GRIT and be Robust enough to stay relatively healthy, alive, and energized, regardless.

That's why it's particularly important and useful to look at the juxtaposition of your GRIT and your Robustness. Of course the main point is, your overall GRIT, and each of these, G-R-I-T and Robustness, can be both permanently and measurably improved.

Quality of GRIT

This portion of your feedback report is intentionally simplified for easy reference. Your report explains to you roughly where you land on these two essential axes or continua. Beyond the scores, you may also wish to consider their interplay, or mix.

For example, a combination of scoring mostly, even modestly, high on A) both Good and Smart GRIT is likely to be superior to being B) exceptionally high on one and low on the other, even if the actual numbers in these two scenarios were equal.

If, however, you are below the midpoint on both, it can substantially hinder the overall effectiveness of relatively Strong GRIT. But if you are fairly Strong, Smart, and Good, you're likely in much more solid shape than someone with bigger fluctuations.

This is why Optimal GRIT means having the best and most Robust combination of Smart, Good, and Strong, across all capacities and contexts. There is an interplay— a combined effect—joining various aspects of GRIT that can transcend basic scores.

As you have discovered, GRIT can be onionesque. As each layer gets peeled, another is revealed. But with your GRIT Gauge feedback, along with the additional insights and examples offered so far, you likely are more than well equipped to progress to take action to **Grow** your GRIT, starting now.

GROW
THE BASICS

"If you want something you've never had, then you've got to do something you've never done."
— UNKNOWN

OK, now that you've Grokked it and Gauged it, you can Grow your GRIT starting now. The tools, or GRIT Gainers™, I've selected for you from our extended menu as the Basics, to get going, are simple, powerful, and agile. You can use them with anyone, including yourself, in any situation, for any goal.

You can use them to get through school more successfully, and radically enhance your chances to graduate and land a great job. You can use them to fortify your health, relationships, and dreams. You can use them to lead others to achieve more than they ever imagined possible. They can also be used at a larger, collective level to make your gritty goals come true. They can be used to help upgrade, even transform your team and organization.

I opened this book with the GRIT Challenge and Khosro Khaloghli's amazing, rags-to-riches story. As KK's wife, Haruka, explains, "Everywhere we go, so many people ask him, 'How can I be more like you?' Or they ask me how they can develop that special element that make KK, KK." What people are really asking is, "How can I craft *my* version of an amazing life (business, family, etc.)?" Wherever you are now, and wherever you want to end up, these tools will help you get from here to there.

Keeping the Sweet Life Sweet

One of my favorite client businesses, whose owners value their privacy, has historically been known for their chocolate. But as sweet as their products may be, it's the life inside the company that has had a particular lure. It is one of those rare places in today's cutthroat global business climate where good people really care about making great products, delighting their customers, and treating everyone right in the process. It's historically been one of those "You're so lucky to work there!" kind of places.

They're pretty much always needing, and at most times trying, to invent and evolve new products as customer tastes change—and to do so at a pace that keeps them in, if not ahead of the game. But chocolate remains a huge part of the business. And some times are sweeter than others.

Lately, for a large part of their business, life's been a little more sour. They've been getting hit from all sides. Premium brands have been nibbling away market share, as the economy rebounds and the appetite for luxury indulgences increases.

As a result, my client did something it rarely ever does. It reduced its workforce to cut costs, at the very time it needed to ramp up its efforts to get back in the black, let alone win. Ouch. Although they implemented their reductions in the most humane and compassionate manner—as is their way—and even though people understood the necessity, it understandably caused cultural tremors and concern. Engagement scores dropped, and morale sagged. For some, especially among the sales teams on the front lines of delivering their numbers, it was pretty devastating.

Companies face these sorts of challenges all the time. It'd be pretty hard to work anywhere for any period of time without facing the tumult of reorganization, rightsizing, reinventing, reconfiguring, realigning, and more. The problem is, as some of my Harvard colleagues will confirm, 75–80 percent of these sorts of change efforts fail or fall short of their intended goal. And they all raise some questions.

At a personal level, how do you maintain morale and hope? How do you dig deep to deliver ever-greater effort when you're losing the battle? How do you lead others to find a way to deliver more with fewer resources? How do you win against competitors that are outspending and outmaneuvering you, at nearly every turn, and stealing your market share in the process? The answer? GRIT.

As the person assigned to equip their sales force will tell you, "There's no question, we provide world-class training. Our sales force is well equipped, which is definitely part of the reason why, over time, we've done so well and grown into one of the largest companies in the world. But world-class sales, relationships, and negotiation skills are no longer enough. We need GRIT! It's not as though we lack it; it's just that we can and need to *improve it*. I'm convinced that, if we can grow and show the right *kind* of GRIT, we'll see some serious gains!" And that's exactly what her team decided to do: go with GRIT.

Here are two of my favorite GRIT Gainers. I've been teaching them at top companies and universities, and with a broad range of clients all over the world. They help anyone and everyone come out on top, to "dig deep and do whatever it takes—even sacrifice, struggle, and suffer—to achieve their most worthy goals in the best possible way."

GRIT Gainer—WhyTry™

"If it scares you, it might be worth a good try."
— SETH GODIN, MARKETING EXPERT, BLOGGER,
BEST-SELLING AUTHOR

Within reason, you can drive a car or ride a bicycle with the wheels out of alignment. Just as any chiropractor will tell you, you can walk when your hip joints are misaligned. Most of us do. But the longer you drive, ride, or walk, and the more out of alignment things become, the more wear and tear you're going to induce, the more you risk collapse, and the more you will compromise your overall journey. The same principle applies to your gritty goals.

It doesn't matter if you're battling to win the chocolate wars or are part of any organization/team trying to win at anything—a soldier fighting in a *real* war, a leader trying to achieve something big, an entrepreneur clawing your way to success, a student scrapping through school to fulfill your dreams, a parent giving your all to raise one or more solid kids, or just a person seriously set on squeezing the most out of life—it still comes down to the alignment between your reason and your effort, or what I call your "Why vs. Try" alignment test. Take this test as the first step, before we boil WhyTry™ down to a simple, portable tool.

You'll want to give this a serious shot. Do your Why vs. Try alignment test now. Here's how. As always, be brutally honest with yourself. Don't offer answers you feel you want or should. Serve up what's real.

1. *Goals*—Quickly jot down your 3–5 most Gritty Goals. These should be your most important and difficult goals. They should require serious effort over time, may come with no guarantee, and you may only have the smallest glimmer of hope for success.

2. *Rank*—Number your goals in order of importance (to you).

3. *Timeline*—Specifically, by when will you achieve each goal?

4. *Why 1–10*—For each gritty goal, ask yourself,

   • "On a scale of 1–10, (10 is strongest possible), how strong is my Why on this goal?" In other words, how genuinely compelled are you to relentlessly pursue this goal? Take note: I'm not asking how strong your Why *should* be; I'm asking how strong it truly is.

5. *Try 1-10*—For each gritty goal, ask yourself, "On a scale of 1–10, (10 is highest imaginable), how strong is my Try on this goal? How much effort and energy does this goal actually consume?" I'm not asking how hard you think, or want others to think, you're working; I'm asking for your honest assessment of how much effort and energy you are pouring into each specific goal.

  - "For the one(s) where my Why exceeds my Try, OR my Try exceeds my Why, how long has that been going on?"

6. *Align*—Which ones are out of whack? Put an "**X**" in this column to indicate those goals that have more than a two-point difference between the Why and the Try.

  - "What is or may become the potential downside of letting that misalignment remain?"

  - "What specific adjustment(s) do I (we) need to make to bring Why and Try into alignment and ideally to their apex (10), on this specific (or any given) goal?"

Goals	Rank	Timeline	Why 1–10	Try 1–10	Align

For each goal you marked with an "X," answer these questions:

1. How long have your Why and Try been out of alignment?

_____

_____

2. What are the downsides of letting that continue?

_____

_____

3. Specifically, what adjustments do I need to make to realign the Why and Try?

_____

_____

You'll notice that it can go both ways. While for most people it's a matter of bringing their Try up to their Why, for others it can be the opposite. Getting the Why up to the Try is essential when you're killing yourself at something that seems pretty worthless. If the Why can't be amped up to the Try, then something has to give.

Likewise, if the Try is comparatively weak, being overshadowed by a stronger Why, then, more often than not, you're going to feel bad. Guilt, remorse, even self-loathing are common cancers that take root at some level when you know you're not putting in nearly enough of the right kind of effort into something that warrants your best. This happens with friendships you value but neglect, with family you ignore or underserve, and all too frequently with spouses or partners who only get the vapors of what's left of you at the end of a grueling week at work or school.

Whys exceed Trys with increasing frequency and intensity at work. If you ask most employees and/or their leaders how many "top priorities" they are supposed to take on, most roll their eyes and laugh. I asked Sharina, a mid-level manager at one of the big health care providers. "Hah!" she roared. "Tell me about it! That's the biggest joke going around here. When you add together what we're mandated from the corporate, regional, and divisional plans, we seriously have seven 'top' priorities. I'm not kidding. It's just frustrating. No one can deliver on everything, so we all just spread ourselves thinner and thinner, knowing we're giving our all, but not delivering our best. It's really hard on people, because they care."

KK *I asked KK about his Why.*

"So, KK. You could have retired decades ago. Tell me honestly, do you even know how much money you have?"

"I have no idea. You see, this is not the thing you focus on. Money is like shadow. You focus on success, on doing something important with your life, and the money it will follow you."

"So right now, every day, you go out of your way to find and give money to the people in the greatest need. What about your money after you're gone? What is your plan?"

He leans in with his most intense gaze. "Paul, you see, on this earth, in this life, there are so many animals and people who cannot help themselves. Old people. They are abused, abandoned. They are alone. They have nothing. I want them to have something. I am leaving all of my wealth to help them."

This is the Why that fuels Khosro's Try.

What about you? Reflect on your GRIT Story. If you had to tell it today, what would it be? And how would you both factor in and describe your WhyTry on what matters most to you?

Right after I concluded a recent GRIT-based session at FedEx's World Headquarters, an IT leader from Europe came up and sort of stood off to the side while I pulled together my belongings to head to the airport. I could tell he wanted to talk. So I stopped, turned, and asked, "Hi, are you by any chance waiting for me?"

"Oh, yes. Thanks. I just wanted to tell you that what we did today completely confirmed a big decision my wife and I have been struggling with lately."

"I'm so glad to hear that," I offered, inviting him to say more.

"You see, we live in the perfect place. It's this gorgeous home, overlooking a park where I can hike and run, in our ideal neighborhood, with lots of fun things we can just walk to, right nearby."

"Sounds amazing."

"It is. But, well, her sister's family and our family are incredibly close. The kids are best friends. And their jobs just don't pay as well. They don't make as much money, and as you say, they have faced plenty of adversity... So we decided to sell our dream house, leave our perfect scenario to create a new one. We found this cul-de-sac where we could live right across from each other and really be part of each other's lives. We could carpool the kids, share groceries, meals, and more. It could be amazing, but it would be a big sacrifice and a lot of work. We're just so comfortable where we are."

"Sounds like you've been giving this a lot of thought."

"Yeah, but it wasn't until today, when you made me confront our Why and our Try, that I realized, for us, the Why is a 10, so the Try should be too."

Why *and* Try. The truth is, for you to show and sustain your best GRIT, you need the best of both. Why and Try have to shine equally bright.

Relational WhyTry

Why limit this tool to just you? Is there any reason you can't use this simple tool with and for others? This is how you ramp it up to the next level(s). Take a key relationship. Similar questions apply.

- What are the top 3–5 things we're striving for in this relationship?
- For each of these, what is our Gritty Goal, the toughest but most important specific thing we are striving to accomplish, and by when?
- Within each Gritty Goal, for you, me, us, how strong is the Why (1–10)?
- Within each Gritty Goal, for you, me, us, how strong is our Try (1–10)?

Then simply do whatever it takes to realign, so your Try and Why are in alignment.

One of the more difficult issues to hash out is when there is a decided difference in the perceived Try. If you perceive your Try to be a ten, and the other person perceives it to be a five, then it might be worth spending a little time exploring and clarifying the discrepancy. The hard part to realize is, you cannot talk someone into his or her Why or Try. But you can ask questions that help that person arrive at a stronger place on either or both.

+Bonus Question—*What adjustments could I/we make to each goal to most dramatically increase the Try or Why, whichever needs it most?*

WhyTry Misalignments

Imagine a work team. My observation from working with and advising countless teams for more than three decades is that most teams operate under a Why vs. Try (W-T) misalignment. This W-T misalignment is one of the most common and perilous drags on organizational momentum. Chances are you've experienced this, at least once, firsthand.

For any team, this misalignment can exist at an individual and/or collective level. Sometimes the misalignment is within or between team members. If you've ever been on a team where you feel your efforts far exceed your Why, you know what I mean. I think of the thousands of people I've met who are working overtime, sacrificing their personal lives for something they essentially think is a waste of time, or worse. Or I hurt for the droves I've encountered who are killing themselves to achieve some goal that is either clearly unattainable or, in their opinion, misguided.

I remember Ann, an executive for a baked goods company, who, in one of her more downtrodden moments said, "So, basically, I commute ten hours per week, to work sixty hours per week, making America fatter. How's that for a legacy?" There are millions of Ann's leaving their loved ones, weaving their way through traffic, and giving the prime energy hours of their lives to something that has lost all meaning.

Likewise, whenever team members have differing views on the perceived importance of the goal or task, or the story they've created around how hard they are working—how much they are sacrificing in the pursuit of that goal—that's WhyTry out of sync.

This was one of the reasons I left academia. I realized that, in relation to many of my colleagues, I was pretty warped. My perception of the Why, the importance of some goals—like creating an amazing, edifying, substantively empowering college experience for our students—was a ten, compared to far too many of the probably more worn down and jaded faculty's two. To me, nothing mattered more. Some who may have started that way, no longer seemed to care. It made me sad for them and the students. Based on the rankings of the allocation of airspace in meetings, college students resided well below earth-shattering issues such as deciding the best way to photocopy syllabi, limiting office hours, or choosing faculty parking spots. We had a discrepancy on Why.

The same discrepancy existed on perceived Try. If you asked me how hard we were trying, how deep we were digging to give our utmost to our students, I honestly would have said, maybe a two or three out of ten. But if you'd heard the way some bemoaned having to be there on a sacred Friday afternoon, or extending one's office hours, you'd think it was a ten. By some of the tenured stalwarts, my perceptions on Why and Try were not well received. I was a cultural outcast, who clearly did not understand "the harsh realities" of university bureaucracy. Perhaps you've had similar, perhaps far tougher "lone voice in the wilderness" experiences.

W-T misalignments can be crippling. As you'll discover in the Advanced Grok chapter, as you make a rung-by-rung rise up the GRIT Ladder, from Individual up through Relational, Team, and Organizational GRIT, the impact can be exponential. In your relationships and your teams, when your Why falls well short of your Try, it's natural to become frustrated, even resentful, and begin to feel like a martyr as you pour your heart and soul into something clearly unworthy.

The same is true when the Try falls well below your Why. You can feel guilty or ashamed for not delivering an effort worthy of the cause. This happens a lot to parents who feel they are putting their all into work with little if anything left for their kids. It's common in overstretched work teams as well. It's not hard to imagine the effect any version of this syndrome has upon overall team/individual engagement and performance, or one's satisfaction with a given relationship.

That's why with every client I've mentioned in this book, or any client I work with, I introduce them to their WhyTry alignment, same as you. Just like the motorcycle racer getting tunnel vision the faster he goes, the more intense things get, the more buried we can get in the weeds. We can lose sight of what mountain we're trying to climb, and why. Have them step back and look at their WhyTry. Then ask them, "For you personally, what is the Why underneath the why?" And then, to bring both parts up to snuff, ask, "What adjustments do you need to make within yourselves to most dramatically strengthen the Try?"

These questions help shore up their WhyTry alignment. The same questions apply in reverse when the Try exceeds the Why.

"You're clearly working really hard at this. Your Try is off the charts. I guess my question is, 'Why are you putting so much into this project?'"

Then, I ask, "And why is that important to you?"

If the answer isn't solid, clear, and convincing, I ask again: "OK, then one more time. Why? What is your reason—the Why—this is worth your greatest effort?"

Sometimes the answer is, because of consequences: "Because if I don't, I'll lose my job!" Well, it may not be a happy reason, but that can be a pretty strong Why!

If they can't come up with a good reason, I ask, "Then why are you killing yourself over this?" Or even, "How can you reroute some of your energy toward more important things, put in less effort on this project, and achieve nearly as good of a result?"

Organizational W-T misalignments are more common than not, and are arguably the single biggest cause of organizational, even cultural, drag. Consider when the General Motors (GM) recall debacle hit and the news of preventable deaths potentially caused by internal denial and delays became public. Look at it through the lens of W-T.

First, there was arguably a difference in the Why, the perceived importance of being obsessed with safety. Some thought it was a ten, others a lot lower. This is not uncommon in many companies, where safety is perceived as an added, if not burdensome, expense, as opposed to a brand-builder and moral imperative.

In the case of GM, some may have understandably put profit at a ten, but maybe not as understandably had safety comparatively, if not dramatically, lower. Whenever there is a perceived trade-off on profitability and safety, and you have people in power who rate those two Whys differently, you have a potential problem.

Second, whenever you hear a top executive say something like, "We gave it our best effort," or "Unfortunately, despite our best efforts, it took us years to figure out the problem," you might be witnessing a fail, or at least a gross misalignment on Try.

Instead, note the GRIT—the clarity and courage—the alignment of Why and Try from CEO Mary Barra: "I realize there are no words of mine that can ease their grief and pain. But as I lead GM through this crisis, I want everyone to know that I am guided by two clear principles: first, that we do the right thing for those who were harmed; and second, that we accept responsibility for our mistakes and commit to doing everything within our power to prevent this problem from ever happening again ... We will not shirk our responsibility."

It's worth noting that, since making that statement, and as the problem and related legal costs continued to significantly worsen, Mary Barra and GM stuck to that promise, showing a gritty level of integrity too rarely found in the news. It's also worth noting that as time goes on, people will A) have at most but a vague memory that GM had some problems, and B) recall almost subconsciously that, unlike the countless sleazier examples, GM took the high road, the GRITty road, took a beating, stood tall, and did it right.

The WhyTry alignment challenge can be an immensely powerful exercise to put yourself and others through. But let's get real. Most of the time, on most days you're moving way too fast to sit yourself down, let alone sit everyone else down and have them thoughtfully write their reflections/answers to each of those questions. You need something you can use right now, with yourself or anyone else, to help you get unstuck from any potentially frustrating moments in pursuit of your goals. That's why I created this and all my other GRIT Gainer Pocket Tools. You can download this one for free. Just search for GRIT™ by PEAK Learning, Inc. in your app store, download, and enjoy.

GRIT App

GRIT GAINER POCKET TOOL
WhyTry™

- **1–10, how strong is my/our/your Why?**
- **1–10, how strong is my/our/your Try?**
- **Specifically, what do I/we/you need to do to maximize and align the Why and the Try?** *(if applicable)*

There's tremendous power in this simple exercise. Aligning your GRIT—your Try with your Why—is one of the most instantly relieving and energizing tools you can employ. When your Try exceeds the Why, you have to ask, well, *why?* In other words, why kill yourself over something that clearly isn't worth it? Realizing this can be a huge relief.

Conversely, when you recognize the gap and upgrade your Try to match your Why, through Smarter, "Gooder," Stronger efforts, it unleashes tremendous determination and energy. You know you are pouring your best efforts into the right pursuits.

Anyone can apply this simple tool. Consider how the WhyTry was recently applied in a team meeting at one of our major media clients who was committed to upgrading the way customers navigated channels and menus (tweaked to protect anonymity).

continued...

And of course, had the team said it was worth pursuing but WhyTry was messed up, the leader would ask, "What adjustments can we make now to truly maximize and align our Why with our Try?"

WhyTry is a simple tool you can apply immediately to demonstrate Smart, Good, and Strong GRIT in your pursuit of any goal. The next tool, the GRIT Goads™, will help you upgrade your G-R-I-T by individual dimensions, and/or across the board.

GRIT Gainer—GRIT Goads™

Overall, making gains on Smart, Good, and Strong GRIT has immense upsides. Nonetheless, there are times when you'll want to delve into the deeper texture by "gritifying" your efforts across one or more of the four dimensions of GRIT—**G**rowth, **R**esilience, **I**nstinct, and **T**enacity. These GRIT Goads are particularly useful for:

A) Focused Improvement—if based on your results from the GRIT Gauge™, you prefer to strengthen one or more specific facets of your GRIT, and/or

B) Situational Application—if you feel a situation warrants addressing and/or shoring up one or more of the dimensions of GRIT.

If you could get inside a gold medal Olympian's brain and extract the three thoughts she has before winning every race, wouldn't you want to know? Likewise, if you could get inside the brain of the person who achieves every goal he sets out to achieve, no matter how bold or daunting, wouldn't you want to put that to use in your own life? These are the questions inside KK's brain when he is in pursuit of any goal, which is pretty much always. It's confirmed. This tool, the GRIT Goads, these questions come the closest to what he asks himself, automatically, to ensure his success.

If there's one thing that messing with nearly a million people (in a good way) for all these years has taught me, it's the power of ask vs. tell. Questions jar the brain, trigger possibilities and pathways that no lecture or advice can match. That's why these GRIT Goads are nothing more than carefully honed, tested, and proven questions that basically serve as field-perfected brain triggers, provoking you to upgrade your GRIT in any situation.

You may apply any or all of these GRIT Goads to any goal or aspiration. And here's the rule: there are no rules! In other words, there are no right or wrong choices. Pick the question(s) or "Goad" that best serves the situation. They all work! However, I strongly suggest that you use them as worded, rather than improvising, at least until you really have these hardwired and mastered.

Goad.
To cause somebody to act.
Synonyms: *Incite, Push, Drive.*

It may seem essentially the same, but there is **actually a huge difference between asking:**

"What research do I need to do, to better understand this situation?"

vs. asking:

"Where can I get the best alternative perspective or insight to better attack this challenge?"

The first is more vague and potentially overwhelming to answer. The second version has more edge, direction, and specificity, and therefore greater actual effect.

GRIT Goads—Full Version

G — Where can I get the best alternative perspective or insight to better attack this challenge?

R — How can I respond even better [and maybe faster] to this situation, so I can move on?

I — What would be an even better approach to achieving this goal?

T — Assuming giving up is not an option, what will I do next, and how soon can I unleash another, upgraded best effort toward this goal, to at least increase my chances of success?

Again, you can substitute "you" or "we" for "I" to effectively apply these GRIT Goads with others. This version tends to work the best, even in everyday conversation with others, one-on-one or in a team. Over time, you'll arrive at a shorthand that everyone who has been along on the GRIT journey will understand.

Imagine the hectic pace and dynamics of the workday. Here's a typical exchange that one leader, who completed our GRIT™ program, reported to me and demonstrated a couple of weeks ago with one of his lead engineers, Rashan, at their regional facility:

continued ...

THAT SOUNDS SMART. HOW SOON DO YOU WANT TO DO THAT?

I'LL PING THEM AS SOON AS WE'RE DONE TALKING. DOES THAT WORK OK?

GREAT! BUT IT SEEMS EVERY TIME WE FACE SOME SORT OF OBSTACLE, WE LOSE STEAM, OR WORSE. HOW COULD WE RESPOND BETTER AND FASTER NEXT TIME, SO WE DON'T GET HELD BACK AND CAN ACTUALLY CONTINUE OUR MOMENTUM?

WE CAN DIVE INTO THE SOLUTION PHASE MUCH FASTER, FOR ONE THING. WE GET SO FIXATED ON HAVING IT ALL PERFECT, RATHER THAN GIVING IT A SHOT AND THEN FIGURING IT OUT AS WE GO.

THAT SOUNDS VERY SMART. I'VE GOT TO HEAD OUT IN A FEW MINUTES. BUT BEFORE I GO, LET ME ASK YOU: IN YOUR OPINION, GIVEN YOUR YEARS OF EXPERIENCE WITH THESE SORTS OF SPECIFICATIONS, WHAT WOULD BE AN EVEN BETTER APPROACH TO ACHIEVING THE GOAL ON THIS DESIGN PROJECT, BEYOND WHAT THE TEAM HAS ATTEMPTED SO FAR?

I THINK WE NEED TO CONSIDER NOT HOW WE MEET, BUT HOW WE DRAMATICALLY EXCEED THE SPECIFICATIONS SO WE BUY SOME COMPETITIVE IMMUNITY, WHICH BUYS US TIME AND PROTECTS OUR PRICING.

I LOVE IT! SO, SINCE, FOR YOU, GIVING UP IS NOT AN OPTION, WHAT WILL YOU DO TO AT LEAST INCREASE YOUR CHANCES OF SUCCESS WITH THIS TEAM ON THIS DESIGN PROJECT?

I'M GOING TO REACH OUT TO MY ENGINEERING COLLEAGUES RIGHT NOW AND SEE WHAT THEY HAVE TO SAY. THEN, WITH YOUR PERMISSION, I'M GOING TO GO INTO OUR NEXT TEAM MEETING, LET THEM KNOW WE TALKED, AND PERSUADE THEM TO RAISE THE BAR, SO WE EXCEED THE KEY SPECIFICATIONS, AND CREATE A TRULY DISRUPTIVE INNOVATION. I THINK THAT COULD WORK!

SOUNDS LIKE YOU'RE ON FIRE! GO FOR IT. LET ME KNOW HOW I CAN HELP.

design by Elizabeth Baniaga

Even the short version of these casual but penetrating goads can work with a schoolmate or friend. GRIT Goads are perfect for those moments when someone you care about is getting demoralized or frustrated, or really for any situation where a dose of greater GRIT could lead to better outcomes. Here's an example, based on a real-time exchange I recently overheard between a couple of students. It was inspiring to witness Brandon practicing this tool immediately following my guest lecture at a well-known East Coast university.

continued...

design by Elizabeth Baniaga

Brandon was simply being a good (and gritty) friend and teammate. The point is, you can apply the GRIT Goads informally and naturally in the course of real conversation with real people to achieve real breakthroughs.

Don't do yourself a disservice by confusing simple with weak. These two simple tools, WhyTry and GRIT Goads, have been pressure tested under every brand of difficult, frustrating, aggravating, hopeless, demoralizing, even life-threatening circumstances, generally creating substantial gains, if not real breakthroughs.

But that's momentary. The enduring effect takes root as you apply these tools within yourself and with others, as frequently as possibly appropriate, day by day, over time. As you literally hardwire this process and mindset, you will discover your GRIT measurably grows. And it's permanent. Once it goes up, it pretty much never sinks back down. These are the Basics of Growing your GRIT. Now, if you're ready, you can turn the page to GROK, GAUGE, and GROW at the Advanced Level, because throughout life, in any and every dimension of it, GRIT Happens!

GROK: To understand something
profoundly and intuitively

You are now equipped to advance your understanding and mastery of GRIT. As you do, the first revelation you've no doubt begun to realize is that GRIT, beneath its rough exterior, is astonishingly, often subtly, multifaceted and multilayered. And it plays out in a broad array of capacities, situations, and levels. It is only from here, by comprehending it from these vantage points, that you can fully appreciate the infused, holographic pervasiveness and power of GRIT. We'll begin with the Four Capacities that shape both your effectiveness and Robustness, then round out the gritscape by examining your various Contexts and rungs up the GRIT Ladder—the ascending levels of positive impact you can generate in your work, life, and beyond.

THE FOUR CAPACITIES OF GRIT

If Optimal GRIT is the single surest path to greatness, then a meaningful part of what it takes to fully live and grow GRIT is to optimize not just the four dimensions, but also the Four Capacities— Emotional, Mental, Physical, and Spiritual—of GRIT. We will therefore upgrade or fill out our definition of Optimal GRIT.

💎 **Optimal GRIT: When you consistently and reliably demonstrate your fullest, "goodest," smartest, and strongest GRIT across all four capacities to achieve your most worthy goals.**

You've no doubt witnessed each of these elements of GRIT in their extremes, as well as the upsides that reveal themselves when all of these are largely in sync—and the downsides when they are not.

It may seem nitpicky, but the reality is, just because a person's overall GRIT may be exceptional (Smart, Good, Strong across G-R-I-T), that does not mean it's emotionally, mentally, physically, and spiritually *balanced*. Most people, on any given day, tend to show more of and less of certain capacities. Being too out of whack can cause the kinds of both short- and long-term problems you most likely see all around you, and have perhaps experienced. The most common is depletion. Statements that people who are depleted may think or say include:

- "I'm exhausted. I honestly don't have the energy to take on one more thing!"
- "My head is going to explode. I'm having enough trouble keeping track of everything, as it is now."
- "I just feel numb. I know I should feel more, but it's just not there."
- "It's getting harder and harder to shore up the hope, faith, and energy to do this."

Depletion has moved to the top of the "Adversities or Challenges in Your Day Job" list, which is compiled from responses to our PEAK survey conducted in every organization we enter. Not only is depletion the most common answer; the intensity of the chorus grows louder. As the world becomes more 24/7, dispassionately demanding, chaotic, frenetic, confusing, and unpredictable, people report being not just tired, but also more comprehensively and deeply depleted. Overdrawing your well to irrigate your crops is not a sustainable solution unless you can bank on plenty of rain.

Depletion often results from the strategic trade-offs we all make. It's difficult, and at times seemingly nearly impossible, not to naturally form warped or imbalanced GRIT. We tend to soar with and depend upon our strengths. And, like the water and crops, we tend to trade whatever we have left over in one category of GRIT to sustain or grow another.

Sometimes these trades pay off with substantial upsides. Although I've never been a fan of this strategy, pouring on more Mental GRIT by cramming for final exams, at the expense of Physical GRIT—too much caffeine, no sleep or exercise, and sheer exhaustion—may result in top marks, followed by the kind of fairly speedy recovery that young bodies somehow repeatedly achieve. And while the ideal is to take even *better* care of yourself during finals, this strategic trade-off may still reward you with an abundant harvest of good marks and a strong GPA.

Sometimes these sorts of trade-offs don't pan out so well. They can bring glaring downsides. More seriously, they can wilt and eventually reduce your overall GRIT. There is growing evidence that the stress hormone cortisol, which elevates with a surge of stress, may actually decrease with chronic stress. The effect may be a delay in, but much greater likelihood of becoming sick.

It appears the protracted struggle one wages on one's body through depletion can backfire in the form of illness, or worse.

That's why part of my not-so-secret agenda with this book is to inspire and equip you to make only (or at least a whole lot more) upside trades—the most necessary and rewarding—vs. any downside trades.

Emotional GRIT, Mental GRIT

When you tell someone, "You're such an amazing and patient listener," you are telling them they demonstrate Emotional GRIT. If Emotional GRIT is about the heart, Mental GRIT is about the mind. Whenever you or someone you know has unwavering, never-ending intensity and focus, chances are you're witnessing an impressive display of Mental GRIT.

> *"Most people do not listen with the intent to understand; they listen with the intent to reply."*
> — STEPHEN R. COVEY, BEST-SELLING AUTHOR OF
> *THE SEVEN HABITS OF HIGHLY EFFECTIVE PEOPLE*

Physical GRIT, Spiritual GRIT

Heart and mind are powerful. But it is the body that so often does the real work and gets things done. People who can deny themselves basic needs— like food, comforts, and shelter—can out-suffer the toughest characters, manage to manufacture unimaginable reserves of energy, or endure the most unspeakable pain are noteworthy for their Physical GRIT. And of course, those rare, largely unknown, Mother Theresa-like characters—or even those pioneering leaders who enter the storm of doubt, evil, darkness, and cynicism in order to bring some modicum of love, hope, and progress to others—are humbly showing us all what Spiritual GRIT is all about.

We speak about GRIT as a single phenomenon, or force. The reality is, GRIT shows up in these four distinct, but often interrelated or connected capacities. Depending on your levels of each, your Emotional, Mental, Physical, and Spiritual GRIT can either cannibalize or feed each other. Once your fuel rods are spent, without being replenished, your reactor can melt down. On the upside, your GRIT capacities can be symbiotic—each feeding the others, and together having them grow stronger, faster, and taller than they ever could on their own.

The goal, if not the imperative, is therefore to strengthen your GRIT across all four capacities, so rather than sap, they can complement, support, and feed each other, across a broad range of circumstances and aspirations. It begins with Grokking and pondering each more deeply.

Grokking Emotional GRIT

Emotional GRIT is what's required to navigate the inevitable disappointments, frustrations, ego blows, and loneliness that arise along most long, arduous journeys. Emotional GRIT is also what enables us humanoids to transcend terror and hopelessness.

Malala Yousafzai was born in 1997 in Pakistan, a hotbed of tumult and danger. Rather than putting her head down to merely survive, this teenager has inspired the world with her fight to make sure every child has safe access to education. She also ignited the Taliban, who—after attacking her bus and shooting her in the head, neck, and shoulder—declared her "the symbol of infidels and obscenity." Malala survived. And she does not relent. Despite countless, ongoing death threats, she perseveres, successfully gathering 2 million signatures for the Rights to Education campaign petition, which led to ratification of the first Rights to Education Bill in Pakistan—the result of exemplary Emotional GRIT.

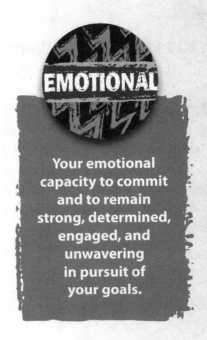

EMOTIONAL

Your emotional capacity to commit and to remain strong, determined, engaged, and unwavering in pursuit of your goals.

"The terrorists thought they would change my aims and stop my ambitions, but nothing changed in my life except this: weakness, fear, and hopelessness died. Strength, power, and courage were born…"

— MALALA YOUSAFZAI, SURVIVOR OF AN ASSASSINATION ATTEMPT BY THE TALIBAN; ACTIVIST FOR WOMEN AND RIGHTS TO EDUCATION; AND AT AGE SEVENTEEN, RECIPIENT OF THE NOBEL PEACE PRIZE

Whenever you've had to endure protracted doubt, worry, concern, or fear—even sleeplessness-inducing excitement and heart-bursting love—you've shown some Emotional GRIT. Entrepreneurs who wake up each day, miraculously converting hope into progress, purpose into profit, and obstacles into opportunities demonstrate the kind of Emotional GRIT that grows jobs, dreams, and economies.

GRIT Challenge—EMOTIONAL GRIT

Right here, in my smallish town of 40,000 residents, a few short miles away from my office is Hathway, a rapidly growing tech firm, or "mobile innovation agency," made up of forty-plus bright young people, providing mobile apps, social platforms, and wearable tech to some of the top companies in the U.S. and overseas. Today, Hathway has earned a spot on the Inc. 5000 as well as the Pac Biz Times 50 Fastest-Growing Businesses. Starting with only a college diploma, how do you create something out of nothing, and within a few short years, become one of the great success stories of your graduating class, as well as one of the more significant employers in your town? Ask Hathway's gritty cofounder and CEO, Jesse Dundon.

"I was once told entrepreneurship means living a few years of your life like nobody wants, so you can live the rest of your life like nobody can," Dundon says. "The emotional roller coaster is incredible. You have to endure the highest highs and definitely the lowest lows. And for a long time, it's a lot more lows than highs. For a year, I lived near Cal Poly, in a converted garden shed behind the garage that housed the first Hathway office. My business partner, Kevin Rice, lived in a converted porch that had a brick BBQ built into one wall at the same house. We didn't move Hathway out of the garage to a real office until it got so cold in the winter that we could barely type. Have you ever tried to type when it's cold enough to see your breath? You have to risk it all, put everything on the line, and give it all you've got. While my friends were seeking security and out having fun, Kevin and I were putting in the hours, living off nothing but hope, and somehow mustering the determination to build the dream. It's brutally tough. That's why it's not for everyone. But I wouldn't trade it for anything!"

Likewise, if you've ever chosen to, or for whatever reason simply been forced to endure an unhappy or abusive relationship, have a terminal or debilitating illness, a dwindling or futile dream, a frustrating, even unbearable job, or a significant financial downturn, you have experienced Emotional GRIT. These are the times you probably wished you had even more of the *right* kind of Emotional GRIT.

A huge role your Emotional GRIT can play is remaining fully committed to those obligations and opportunities that once made your heart race and now make your heart heavy. This is true at work and beyond. Anyone can get excited about "new." A new opportunity, new location, new adventure, new job, new responsibility, new role, even a new routine can get the juices flowing enough to make you show up with your best stuff. The test is, how well and to what extent do you continue to show your best stuff over time, long after the glossy veneer of "new" has worn off? It is this capacity—to show the Emotional GRIT to bring your best, day in and day out, at the same level of intensity and passion on Day 427 as you did on Day 1—that so often makes the difference between normal and great.

> *"I learned that courage was not the absence of fear, but the*
> *triumph over it. The brave man is not he who does not*
> *feel afraid, but he who conquers that fear."*
> — **NELSON MANDELA, NOBEL PEACE PRIZE WINNER**
> **AND FORMER PRESIDENT OF SOUTH AFRICA**

With marriages on the wane and divorces continuing a general rise, one could argue that there is a drop-off of Emotional GRIT. One reason for the nation-threatening and troubling drop in (and aging of) the population in Japan is a growing disinterest in intimacy. There is even a name for this syndrome, *sekkusu shinai shokogun,* which translates to "celibacy syndrome." Sixty-one percent of men and 49 percent of women ages eighteen to thirty-four are not in any kind of romantic relationship, with 45 percent of women and 25 percent of men having a complete disinterest in, or distaste for, sex. According to relationship counselor Ai Aoyama, "Relationships have become too hard." Many teenagers prefer the simplicity of the virtual world over the "complexifications" of the real world. Simplicity, comfort, and ease are the seductive sirens that lure us from a potentially much more emotionally gritty and gritifying path.

Emotional GRIT is also both hugely valued and sometimes alarmingly absent at work. I keep waiting for Gallup's annual and growing poll of 25 million workers in 189 countries to show a positive trend shift. But among their three categories, "engaged," "not engaged," and "actively disengaged," 70 percent of employees live many of the prime hours of their lives on the dark side, being at least partially, if not actively disengaged, costing the U.S. economy roughly half a trillion dollars per year. Both bosses and employees clearly play a role.

The reality for most of us with jobs is, there will be at least occasional, if not a relentless barrage of disappointments, setbacks, heartaches, frustrations, deceits, conflicts, complexities, changes, and insanities. For many, their jobs consist of little else. It might be relevant and worth repeating my earlier-reported finding that 98 percent of employers would hire based on GRIT over perfect qualifications, and why they would trade 7.3 "normal employees" for just one with impressive GRIT.

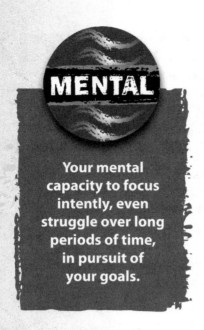

Your mental capacity to focus intently, even struggle over long periods of time, in pursuit of your goals.

Grokking Mental GRIT

If you're a boss or one who leads others, how dare you (or how dare I, as a leader and boss) require greater Mental GRIT of our people than we demonstrate ourselves. To be true leaders, we must set the bar, be the exemplars for our followers and team members to both illuminate what's possible and to make sure there is some genuine integrity in the standards we set for others.

Although bound to a wheelchair, crippled with ALS (a form of motor neuron disease), Stephen Hawking stands among the tallest on Mental GRIT. Sheer intellect mental horsepower doesn't hurt. But tackling and decoding some of the most complex, protracted, intractable mysteries of the universe requires Mental GRIT. It is only through his relentless, almost tireless intensity, focus, and effort that he arrives at the most comprehensive theories and explanations of the universe-for-the-common-person ever published.

> *"My goal is simple. It is a complete understanding of the universe, why it is as it is and why it exists at all."*
> — STEPHEN HAWKING, THEORETICAL PHYSICIST

Whenever you see someone with the most intense, unwavering, undying focus, you are witnessing Mental GRIT. Whenever you see someone stick with, muck through, hack away at, and slowly unravel the gnarliest complexities, you are seeing Mental GRIT in action. And whenever you fend off fatigue, competing stimuli, and more seductive distractions in order to remain fully present and engaged—or to separate important from unimportant, fact from fiction, goal from distraction—you are showing your Mental GRIT as well. Like most capacities, the more you flex it, the more Mental GRIT grows.

Mental GRIT has renewed cachet. The more besieged we are with technology-induced seductions—demanding nanosecond attention spans—the more precious and rare becomes our authentic, deep, whole-brained focus, presence, understanding, and thoughts. And the murkier and muckier our problems, the more precious mental stamina and GRIT become.

KK *Mind over matter is a daily discipline, just like working out in the gym, says KK. "It becomes a habit; if you use your mental capacity or mental power or control, it becomes stronger and stronger through the years. It takes many years. I had to learn to concentrate. It's hard! I had to learn mental discipline. As a child, I had to divide the bread into five pieces for five people in family. It was a system. I use systems, this discipline, for everything."*

• • • • • • • • •

The idea or question may have already sparked in your brain. So, I suppose I would be remiss not to comment on what happens to Mental GRIT when our devices become our vices. On one hand—given that our tech tools in general are quite literally reshaping our brains and distracting us from minor responsibilities, like driving—clearly, the luxury of intense, protracted focus has all but dropped off the map. Or has it?

Ever play a ridiculously cool video game or try to interrupt someone while they are "in battle"? If television at its very best is mesmerizing, some video games go beyond by becoming immersive, engaging, and captivating. Going without food, water, and often bathing is legend among dedicated gamers.

I offer this as proof that it is not the device itself that kills or enhances GRIT, but how we use it. It takes a lot of Mental GRIT just to set aside the game or device, or to ignore the tempting text that just pinged your Pavlovian response into high gear.

The nanosecond, blazing-thumbs, micromessaging way more and more people communicate has definitely shifted the way people connect. There is more surface and less depth; communication has become radically briefer and shallower. Not exactly a boost to Mental GRIT. On the other hand, is there any reason you can't use a smartphone to demonstrate some Smart GRIT?

When you use a device to accelerate and improve your path and progress from here to there, chances are, you are showing Smart GRIT. When you use your device to gather alternative perspectives, add vital wisdom, and explore fresh alternatives, that's a good start. Committing to work as long, hard, and Smart as necessary to arrive at the best conclusions goes further on the Mental GRIT scale.

GROK—ADVANCED

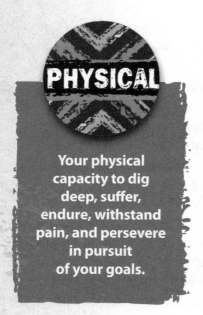

PHYSICAL

Your physical capacity to dig deep, suffer, endure, withstand pain, and persevere in pursuit of your goals.

Grokking Physical GRIT

You can immediately think of someone who is known, if not famous, for his or her raw, Physical GRIT. Maybe that person is you. Physical GRIT is not always as obvious as the marathon runner limping across the finish line in exquisite agony. It's often hidden from view.

GRIT Challenge—PHYSICAL GRIT

Sue Schneider (fake name to protect her privacy) suffers chronic, 24/7, unrelenting, peel your skin off and run off a cliff kind of pain. As part of my GRIT Challenge, I literally walked down the street and met a guy in the local surf shop who turns out to be a well-known "pain doc" in the area. He told me about Sue because he said of all his patients she is the grittiest. Just getting out of bed requires a greater dose of suffering than most of us can bear. It takes her fifteen to thirty minutes.

Even after being diagnosed with and overcoming three forms of supposedly terminal cancer, living with severe, nearly crippling rheumatoid arthritis, having shingles, and suffering the worst migraine headaches he's ever seen, where just opening her eyes can cause writhing agony, she does whatever it takes to fully participate in society, when most people would be bedridden on medications, if not suicidal.

"Here's the crazy part," the doc added. "Although most people would be laid out on a morphine drip, with Sue, on most days, she's up and about. I mean, you'd never know. She just refuses to give in to her pain... For example, even though preparing a meal is sheer torture, like almost impossible to perform, she somehow works through the pain to cook for her family and be there for her kids."

The ability to physically endure the most unspeakable pain, suffering, hardships, conditions, challenges, and burdens has been the guts of human legend from ancient scripture, through Greek mythology, up to the warfare, refugee camps, ghettos, famines, and natural disasters we witness worldwide today. Seeing the astonishing Physical GRIT in others is what inspires us to go beyond what our own comfort-seeking instincts tell us is acceptable. There's a reason why the world is collectively drawn to their screens every four years as the Olympic Games highlight the most breathtaking, inspiring stories of those who've endured and sacrificed the most to become the best.

Sadly, there are times—and for many of us, there comes *a* time—when the body simply cannot manufacture what's required. It lacks the persistence that the mind, heart, and spirit may have joined forces to determinedly require. Such imbalance is hardly reserved for the elderly or frail. Fatigue, illness, and genetics, not to mention life circumstances, can and often do impose real, potentially frustrating limitations on even those with otherwise exceptional Mental, Emotional, and Spiritual GRIT. As any Olympian will tell you, Physical GRIT goes far, but it seldom operates, and is almost never optimized, in isolation.

Grokking Spiritual GRIT

Whenever your faith, values, purpose, commitment, and tenacity are endlessly challenged, even assaulted beyond measure, it is Spiritual GRIT that must prevail. Whenever you find yourself required to truly sacrifice, endure, and/or suffer—as we all eventually do— you are tapping your Spiritual GRIT to rise up and forge onward. It is your Spiritual GRIT that determines your ability to transcend, to rise above everyday—as well as the most crippling—versions of injustice, hardship, pain, disappointment, frustration, apathy, and loss.

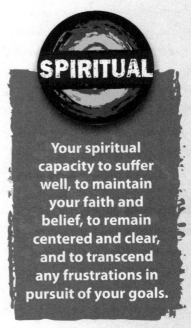

Your spiritual capacity to suffer well, to maintain your faith and belief, to remain centered and clear, and to transcend any frustrations in pursuit of your goals.

Few can match the Fourteenth Dalai Lama as an exemplar. Imagine, for your entire life, being banished from your homeland, forbidden from living your holy destiny, and being forced to watch your people and all that you love be subjugated to contrary, even brutal rule. Consider what it takes to not just endure, but also to transcend it all, emerging not with cynicism or bitterness, but serving as a beacon of happiness, forgiveness, humility, and joy to the world, until your final breath.

"There is a saying in Tibetan, 'Tragedy should be utilized as a source of strength.' No matter what sort of difficulties, how painful experience is, if we lose our hope that's our real disaster."

— DALAI LAMA XIV, TIBETAN BUDDHIST MONK, AUTHOR OF THE ART OF HAPPINESS

We do a very tactile exercise in our GRIT programs, involving colored stones that represent the different capacities. People determine, 1) compared to the exemplars, how much of each capacity they possess, and 2) where and how much of each they actually invest at work or school vs. everywhere else—which is labeled "personal." It's a humbling and enlightening challenge. People first have to come to grips with whatever limitations they may have in the four specific capacities, and then how well or poorly they allocate these—and who gets what from them as a result—according to what really matters most.

Clearly, the ideal is to have a strong, relatively even balance between the four capacities. This is how you achieve the most impossible goals. It was on her fifth attempt over thirty-three years, and at the age of sixty-four, that Diana Nyad became the first person to complete the 110-mile swim across the shark-infested waters from Cuba to Florida (without a shark cage). It took her fifty-three hours, a physical feat almost beyond comprehension. But when asked, Diana cited the strength of her mind, heart, and spirit as what allowed her to do what her twenty-eight-year-old body failed to accomplish. For Diana Nyad, achieving her dream, going the distance, while enduring such exhaustion, hunger, and pain—being mercilessly stung by jellyfish almost the entire way—was clearly accomplished through the exceptional and powerful interplay of all four GRIT capacities. That same interplay is what can fuel your dreams too.

"The spirit is larger than the body. The body is pathetic compared to what we have inside us."

— DIANA NYAD, WHO SWAM 110 MILES FROM CUBA TO FLORIDA, AT AGE SIXTY-FOUR

SITUATIONAL GRIT

Rather than asking yourself, "Where do I spend my time?" consider asking yourself, "Where do I invest my *GRIT*?" For all sorts of reasons, if you are like most people, you probably demonstrate not just imbalanced, but also uneven or inconsistent GRIT. Chances are, you aren't as gritty in some situations as others. That's entirely normal. At times, it might even be smart. Other times, it can prove unfortunate. What has been a missing part of the "grit 1.0" or generic grit conversation is the simple, frank reality that people demonstrate different levels of grit in different contexts and moments. Think about how profoundly that basic truth plays out in your life, work, and pursuits—as well as those of the people around you.

💎 **Optimal GRIT:** When you consistently and reliably demonstrate your fullest, "goodest," smartest, and strongest GRIT across all four capacities and all **worthwhile situations** to achieve your most worthy goals.

To fully grok how Situational GRIT plays out, you may wish to draw your own GRIT Contexts. The ones in the diagram above are simplified. They are generic and condensed. Within relationships, for example, you may have family, friends, boyfriend, girlfriend, club, team, spouse or partner, and others. Likewise, you might have several dimensions of community, including volunteering, synagogue, church, events, causes, memberships, organizations, outreach, and more. Some people even have multiple contexts for work. The more you personalize this model, the more powerfully informative—and for most people both humbling and inspiring—it becomes.

As you lay yours out, even at a quick glance you realize that a perfectly even distribution of GRIT across all contexts is rare, if not nearly impossible. It may not even be desirable. Some people are grittier at work than at home. Some show their best stuff at the gym but become gritless on the job. A specific hobby or interest might garner one's greatest GRIT. Others seem to funnel all they have into key relationships, like closest friends and family, with little left over for anyone and anything else. Sometimes life simply demands a deliberate GRIT shift.

GRIT Challenge—GRIT SHIFTS

Paul Brown is an exceptionally bright-eyed and bright-minded, talented graduate of the local university, who, during a weak job market, landed a dream career at EY (Ernst & Young) in San Francisco. After several months of giving them his best efforts and hours, he realized it was someone else's dream job, not his. "I feel compelled to serve my country. I've been so blessed; it just seems like something I should do," he explains. So, after a year of paying his dues, he rerouted, left EY, and moved away from home so he could train his hardest to win a spot as an officer in the U.S. Marines. He needed two things as he prepared for his challenge: money to pay his bills and a schedule that allowed enough time to train.

"I have taken a couple of retail clerk jobs, which should be pretty simple, so I can really put my mind, body, and spirit into my hours of daily training, not into my job. I won't get rich, but I can focus on what matters most to me for the next several months."

Some people—like students who are put on academic probation, or employees given their final warning from their boss for underperforming—are forced to create a GRIT shift, or else. However, the most positive GRIT shifts occur when they are deliberate (by choice) and values-driven.

Tina Miller has been a phenomenal member of the PEAK Team for fourteen years. Along the way, she created a GRIT shift. For years, she worked way too many hours, pouring a disproportionate (but appreciated) chunk of her GRIT into her job and our purpose-rich practice.

As with so many parents-to-be, when she became pregnant with her first child, priorities—where she invested much of her Emotional, (maybe not as much Mental), Physical, and Spiritual GRIT—had to shift. She knew she had to be not just a gritty PEAKer but also, more importantly, a gritty parent. Tina now appropriately funnels the same Growth, Resilience, Instinct, and Tenacity she shows at work into nurturing her three lucky children. She continues to contribute immensely to our work, but flexibly scheduled part time, with a much more sustainable and healthful, values-driven distribution of her considerable GRIT.

Consider how Situational GRIT plays out at work. If you've ever walked through or been part of a workplace, you have probably witnessed countless creative ways people invest time but little or no GRIT. Last I checked, I think it's called "slacking," "putting in seat time," or in the PEAK vernacular, "camping" vs. "climbing." Performance ratings at work, just like grades in school, are not based upon time invested, but upon *results*.

I can't even begin to count the thousands of frustrated managers and frontline employees I've run into who feel required to dig deep and give their all to tasks and projects that are clearly not high priority to them, but may be to their customer or their boss. A huge part of the frustration is, whatever GRIT they have misspent is GRIT that can no longer be better spent.

Sasha Ramchandani was head of finance for a division at a large insurance company. When the CEO proclaimed he wanted much tighter, more detailed reporting to assist leaders in making more informed decisions regarding strategy and resources, Sasha took it to heart. She imposed huge new reporting requirements on her entire staff. The reports were highly complex and difficult to assemble. They were both time- and GRIT-consuming. Everyone was cranking long hours, racking their brains, trying to figure out how to gather and report the data required in the new reports. This became their new normal.

The problem was, this new requirement, which created reams of additional detail, went so far beyond what busy leaders could ever afford to scrutinize that it became nearly useless. And, of course, pouring their Mental and to some degree Physical GRIT into that one task left them with little for the long list of arguably more important tasks that kept the rest of the business running.

• • ▪ ▪ • ● • •

Here's a simple rule of thumb: Over time, the degree to which your GRIT maps with the strategic priorities of the organization is the degree to which your boss is likely delighted with you and your performance. Put another way, assuming that (unlike my prior faculty example) the priorities are relatively virtuous, *align your GRIT with what matters most, and everyone wins.*

Doesn't the same rule apply to your personal life? Isn't the degree to which your GRIT aligns with what matters most the degree to which you and everyone involved in your life benefit? Conversely, when you invest not just your time, but also your GRIT in low-priority tasks, distractions, or people, doesn't that by definition rob from more worthy pursuits and people?

GRIT Challenge—MISALIGNMENTS

At a fundraiser for the local animal shelter, I ended up talking to Jenny, an acquaintance I'd chatted with at prior gatherings. I knew she was nice, but I did not know she was an "Ironman widow." Don't worry. I didn't know what the term meant either until Jenny explained. We were perusing the items for auction, one of which was a vacation getaway to Hawaii.

"I'd love to go for that one," she sighed.

"Well, why don't you? I promise I won't outbid you!"

"Hah. I'm a total Ironman widow! I'd bid, but it's just that Tom puts in four to six hours per day training for that stupid race. And then he can spend another couple of hours at night studying or preparing for it. He's super committed. Has been for years. I swear, sometimes it's like I hardly see him. So what's the point of being alone there [pointing to the eye-popping picture of the Hawaiian coast] vs. here?"

"Wow, that's serious dedication!"

"Yeah, I don't mean to sound bitter, but sometimes I wish he would put that kind of energy into our marriage! It's not just the time. Really. I'm OK with that. But by the time he gets home, he's shot. It's like he leaves his best stuff out there [waving her arm across the landscape] and has none of it left for here," she explained, gesturing back and forth to indicate between two people.

● ● ● ● ● ● ● ●

Jenny was clearly wishing her husband would make a GRIT shift. One of the most powerful shifts you can make right now is to put less focus on where and how you and those around you spend time, and more on where you and they invest GRIT. The stronger that maps to what matters most, the more everyone wins.

You can take on the GRIT Shift challenge now. What is one area of your life/work that deserves more of your best energy than it currently gets? Conversely, what is one area that maybe gets more than it deserves? If you could make a single GRIT Shift, shifting your best energy and GRIT from one area to another, what would it be?

THE GRIT LADDER

GRIT is about not just dreaming, but actually doing—relentlessly pursuing and achieving your best goals, in the best ways. GRIT is about your immediate and long-term impact. It is what fuels and determines how much of a difference you make in whatever time you have left.

Throughout this book you've learned how others use GRIT to fuel their effectiveness and contribution at all levels. You can sense how that creates a flywheel of new opportunities-fueled-by-contribution-fueled-by-GRIT, fueling new opportunities... and so on.

Since GRIT is all about impact, it's important and useful to consider how that impact tends to increase in ascending orders of magnitude, like climbing the rungs of a ladder. It begins with your first step, which is: the GRIT Ladder.

◆ Optimal GRIT: When you consistently and reliably demonstrate your fullest, "goodest," smartest, and strongest GRIT across all four capacities, all worthwhile situations, and **every rung** to achieve your most worthy goals.

SOCIETAL

ORGANIZATIONAL

TEAM

RELATIONAL

INDIVIDUAL

ASCENDING LEVELS OF GRIT

Individual GRIT

Think about that one thing in your life for which you have sacrificed the most over the longest period of time, perhaps struggled and suffered deeply, to make happen. That's where the GRIT Ladder begins.

You. You are the main focus of and a large chunk of the motivation for this book. You're where it all starts, by Grokking, Gauging, and Growing your personal GRIT. I want you to enjoy the rich, far-reaching benefits that come from fortifying all facets of your life with greater GRIT. But I must also confess: the rest of the reason for this book is because "you"—that includes the collective "you"—are the foundation of even grander GRIT.

As you ascend rungs, your potential impact multiplies exponentially. With that comes the opportunity for this work to have the kind of larger-scale effect any self-respecting researcher/author with a reasonable (or perhaps unreasonable) blend of aspiration and delusion is likely to pursue. None of the other rungs exist, or can even begin to be optimized, without Individual GRIT. And since each rung elevates your impact, I challenge you to embrace an even fuller definition of Optimal GRIT.

> Your **contribution** "out there" will never exceed your **GRIT** "in here."

"Unless you're a genius, I don't think that you can ever do better than your competitors without a quality like grit."
— MARTIN E.P. SELIGMAN, DIRECTOR OF THE UNIVERSITY OF PENNSYLVANIA'S POSITIVE PSYCHOLOGY CENTER

Relational GRIT

If you've ever seen a marriage disintegrate, you may have witnessed a collapse of Relational GRIT. The dream of an enduring love, a great life, financial security, amazing children, and the tail-wagging golden retriever may be cliché. But making it all happen typically takes a lifetime of effort and sacrifice. It takes GRIT. That's one reason relationships so often fail. And it's also one reason they can be massively rewarding. When two or more people combine their GRIT toward shared goals, it can be amazing.

Because of its potency, your increasingly Strong, Smart, Good (Optimal) GRIT will inevitably serve as a positive and powerful contagion. That's tremendously exciting! It will profoundly or subtly influence others, as well as the strength and duration of your bonds with them. That is why Individual GRIT almost invariably fuels Relational GRIT.

Relational GRIT has two parts. It is both an infuser and a shaper. By "infuser," I mean the ways in which your GRIT influences other people's GRIT. Your GRIT gets inside their mindset, affecting or infecting how others think and behave. This often happens subconsciously, much the way another person's energy can so infectiously affect yours.

The implications as a parent, friend, colleague, sibling, community member, and leader are immense. The moment your GRIT affects another is the moment you've amplified your Individual GRIT to Relational GRIT. This is arguably one of the greatest honors and opportunities GRIT bestows on us all. Quite honestly, if you close this book and focus on that one thing—using your smartest, "goodest," strongest personal GRIT to help generate that in others— you will have an immense, enduring impact, as well as a deeply "gritifying" life.

GRIT serves as a "shaper" by inevitably defining much of what forms an enduring, and one hopes endearing, relationship. The richest elements of human bonds, the stuff you care about most—respect, trust, humor, inspiration, and love—can all be radically influenced, if not utterly determined by the GRIT of those involved. How well do you really respect that gritless person who folds every time things get the least bit tough? How much do you trust the person who crumbles in the face of adversity? And how close, let alone dependent, are you willing to be with someone with a noxious combination of Bad, Dumb, and Low GRIT?

You've no doubt experienced the shift that occurs when the individuals' GRIT Mixes are transcended, and pure Relational GRIT kicks in. Now it's no longer about you and yours; it's about us and ours. For example, in our marriage, for Ronda and me, the question becomes how well and to what extent do we, *as a couple,* dig deep and do whatever it takes—even sacrifice, struggle, and suffer—to achieve worthy goals, together? To what extent do we demonstrate Growth, Resilience, Instinct, and Tenacity across all contexts and situations? How well do we err toward Smart and Good over Dumb and Bad GRIT? The answers to these questions are different from—and trump—what happens individually.

For some people, Relational GRIT surpasses, even far exceeds the combination of their Individual GRIT. Something about the magic of being together engenders a level of courage, tenacity, and aspiration that at a personal level simply doesn't exist. For other people, it's the inverse. For whatever reason(s), the relationship's GRIT is far weaker and worse than that of either member. The relationship makes each person less, rather than more.

I've been recently coaching a global top executive who faced this exact scenario. In their relationship, he had exceptional GRIT—Good, Smart, and Strong. That's clearly part of what makes him such a universally respected and adored leader. She did not. Her relational GRIT was more moderate and mixed. Separately, the same held true. But together, they could not achieve even the average, let alone the best of the blend. Together, their GRIT was not as Smart, Good, and Strong as the mix might suggest, or as you might guess if you knew both partners. She had a history of moments of Bad and/or Dumb GRIT, from which he would fight to help them recover. It was a pattern on which she relied.

Finally, a moment of Bad/Dumb GRIT took its toll. Rather than digging deep and doing whatever it takes to create an exceptional marriage and raise great kids, she made some decidedly weak, selfish, and devastating choices, which shattered their union and tore apart the family. Separately, things are arguably better. His Good, Strong, and Smart GRIT is setting him and his children on a path toward actually emerging better and stronger because of the adversity, while her lesser GRIT can impose less overall damage. This sort of scenario is not terribly uncommon.

I have become increasingly convinced that GRIT is what determines whether a relationship is healthy or sick, good or bad, energizing or depleting, lasting or fleeting, worthwhile or not. If together, you and I exercise Strong, Good, and Smart GRIT, nothing can stop us, and we're likely to find our friendship immensely energizing and rewarding. We are likely to trust, respect, and seek each other out, because together, we can accomplish some great things we might not accomplish solo, and because we know the other person is doing everything in their power to make sure what they do is ultimately beneficial to the other.

Conversely, if individually we each have decent GRIT, but together we somehow end up pursuing wimpy things in wimpy ways, or worse yet, pursuing damaging things in stupid ways, I'm going to make a wild guess that our friendship has a short shelf life. In these ways, and countless others, GRIT shapes the nature, quality, experience, and duration of relationships. A few, particularly choice friendships from high school and/or college might come to mind!

Team GRIT

Today, more and more business customers are served by a team. In the "CPG" (Consumer Packaged Goods) realm—which includes everything packaged that you buy in stores like the Walmarts, Tescos, Targets, Costcos, PetSmarts, Krogers, and Safeways of the world—they don't want to be served by a bunch of individuals from a given vendor, each with their own approach and solutions. They don't have the time or bandwidth for that.

Nearly all clamor for a team, with one voice and one unified solution to make things simple, good, and profitable. And they clamor for GRIT. Almost—or sometimes completely—trumping pure price, they crave the partners/vendors who will dig deep and do whatever it takes—even struggle, sacrifice, and suffer—to get them what they need and fulfill the promises they make.

When you think of all the teams you've ever been a part of, which one would you say demonstrated the greatest GRIT? Which one dug the deepest to achieve the most worthwhile goals? If you applied the same question to athletic teams, which one would you choose? Assuming you could come up with one, the memories of that team would instantly elevate you.

Or, if you're like me, maybe you've been part of that tragic human experiment, when you take a bunch of good people with reasonable GRIT, throw them together on a team, and watch them implode. My eighth-grade ice hockey team, with the not terribly original name the "Blackhawks," had some incredibly talented players. I was not among that group. And we had a lot of players with gobs of GRIT. In the tryouts, which were extremely arduous, given that we were in the part of the country where a lot of high schoolers go pro, the coach was exceedingly deliberate in picking the hardest workers, who showed the greatest hustle. I was lucky he valued GRIT as much as talent.

The short version is, in spite of all our potential, we couldn't buy a victory. We were pathetic. And the tougher the game, the worse we played. Whenever we were behind, or in a real clinch, we fell apart. Together, we became less, not more. Blame, anger, and apathy infected the entire squad and probably our poor parents. It was like cancer. As the interminable season wore on, many of the friendships on the team disintegrated, and the original joy of being part of a team morphed into utter dread. We couldn't wait for it to end.

Beyond the sum of the individuals, and often trumping their relationships, Team GRIT kicks in. And it exercises its influence in any and all teams, whether for sports, work, family, community, or school. As with the prior level, Team GRIT shapes and determines the nature, potential, and success of the team.

In business, Team GRIT, over Individual GRIT, is what every leader counts on for the key strategic projects and initiatives to be successfully completed. Without a solid serving of GRIT, how do teams navigate the seemingly endless frustrations and complexities to imagine, design, invent, engineer, produce, market, sell, and support a promising new product or service in time to gain any competitive advantage?

In any long-term business relationship, despite your team's absolute best efforts to make everything go right, you can be sure the day will come when something, or maybe many things, go wrong. It is Team GRIT, over Individual GRIT, that will determine the speed and quality of the response, as well as the quality of the relationship, going forward. It is Team GRIT that wins or loses the next contract. And it is the strength of relationships between gritty individuals that forms the team. In this sense, the economic value of exceptional—when compared to poor—Team GRIT is safely in the hundreds of billions of dollars.

How much Smart vs. Dumb GRIT does your team show? Do you consistently pursue the best things in the smartest ways? Or do you occasionally pursue less-than-ideal goals in less-than-optimal ways?

Have you ever been part of a team that unintentionally (or intentionally) showed Bad GRIT? When one of the media giants asked me in to do some work for them, the boss pointed at the CTO (Chief Technology Officer) and said, "Mike, I'm going to ask Paul to help you fix your team." When I asked what the problem seemed to be, before Mike could say a word, the alpha dog boss barked, "They're the goddamn business prevention department! Everything we ask for, they either tell us why it can't be done or take six times longer than necessary to deliver it, at which point it's likely to be friggin' obsolete!" Mike looked like a whipped dog.

When I got some "us" time with Mike, he explained why the boss was so irate. Mike had spent a ton of money bringing in some hot talent to do a massive system upgrade throughout the whole global business. "We were all so excited. And personally, I saw this as our finally having an opportunity to stop being seen as a repair shop, and start being seen as a real strategic business partner."

Their intentions were good. But their results were seriously damaging. The system implementation was an unmitigated disaster. It brought the business to its knees, all but killing people's ability to communicate, let alone work. People were like tsunami survivors, texting each other information on cell phones, to at least know their coworkers and projects were alive.

Bosses throughout the business went rogue. They unplugged and mothballed the corporate solution, and went out and bought their own, so their people could actually get stuff done and help the business survive the sinkhole the now infamous tech team had created. Good intentions gone very bad. That's Bad GRIT at the Team level. All the tools I offer you to Grow GRIT, both Basic and Advanced, can be used to help you avoid this pitfall.

Of course anyone who has been on many teams has witnessed, even contributed to Dumb GRIT. If I had a dollar for every time, at some client organization, I've heard some version of, "Well, we've been working on this forever!" or, "We been at this for years. And I guess we'll just keep plugging away," I could buy every leader in the world a copy of this book!

Organizational GRIT

The Sebastian Hotel in Vail, Colorado, has the brand promise "Ask and consider it done." That's a big promise for that single property to fulfill. Wolfgang Neumann, CEO of hospitality giant Carlson Rezidor, kicks that promise up several notches.

He has intentionally and determinedly set forth to create what he calls a "Yes!" culture, one where all employees from the front to the back of the house emphatically say "Yes!" to whatever guests request, then demonstrate the Individual and Team GRIT to go make it happen. As he explained to his top 350 leaders, "Giving guests whatever they want, no matter how difficult, making the impossible possible ... that will be our competitive advantage." That requires Strong, Good, and Smart GRIT. The ideal is Optimal GRIT—having the best version of GRIT show up across all situations, levels, and more. The fact that Wolfgang Neumann scores in the top few percentiles on GRIT is likely no coincidence, and no small factor in Carlson Rezidor's chances of success.

Strong or Weak, Good or Bad, Smart or Dumb, the consequences of GRIT get intensified and amplified at the organizational level. Just as every organization has its own personality, culture, climate, and vibe, every organization has its own brand of GRIT. In fact, beyond the GRIT sum of its individuals, relationships, and teams, Organizational GRIT is arguably the key shaper of each of the elements listed in the prior sentence. Does your organization have a Strong GRIT or Weak GRIT culture? Is it perceived as gritty or wimpy?

If you could choose between an organization with Optimal GRIT vs. the one utterly lacking, where would you prefer to work? Whose products or services would you purchase? Which would earn your loyalty? Whose stock would you buy?

Organizational GRIT determines pretty much everything, especially over time. It is a key factor in what and how much an organization decides to pursue. It determines the boldness, magnitude, and nature of their vision and strategic plan. It shapes what they intend to become and what they are about. It informs their mission and purpose. GRIT determines how well and to what degree any organization lives up to its values, principles, and brand promise. Without GRIT, these become slick marketing campaigns, at best, or more likely than not, a series of shattered covenants. GRIT is also what determines not just how well they survive, but also how well they take advantage of— and emerge stronger and better from—even the most devastating economic downturns and events.

It's important to realize that much like Team and Relational GRIT, Organizational GRIT relies upon and cannot exceed, but can potentially fall below, the combined levels of Individual, Relational, and Team GRIT within its world. This is what can keep CEOs and top executives up at night. How do you not just get people to believe, but also to actually demonstrate GRIT, collectively and individually, in pursuit of your most ambitious goals?

That is exactly why you will want to learn and begin to master **Gritty Goals** and the **Gritty Game Plan** tools in the **Grow–Advanced** section of this book. These will help you to literally gritify what you go after and how you go after it. At the end of the day, fiscal year, and lifespan, your organization's, *any* organization's capacity to dig deep and do whatever it takes—even struggle, sacrifice, and suffer—to fulfill its boldest aspirations is what largely determines its destiny.

Societal GRIT—Good

Five-year-old Miles Scott was in remission from leukemia. His obsession with comic book heroes sparked the Make-A-Wish Foundation to turn part of San Francisco into Gotham City, so Batkid (Miles) and a full-sized Batman could pull up in a Batman-decaled Lamborghini and foil their archnemesis, the Penguin, by liberating a burgled bank vault and other feats. More than 7,000 people, many with cameras, filled the streets to see and help Miles' vision come to life. Within days, tens of thousands, maybe hundreds of thousands of people worldwide were sporting Batkid T-shirts and making their $20 donations to the Make-A-Wish Foundation.

Likewise, the globally viral online phenomenon called "The Ice Bucket Challenge" has raised more than $120 million for the ALS Association, for research and cures for that debilitating neurological disease. While its origin is unclear, the path of Individual to Societal GRIT and Good is uncontested. Sometimes "getting there," the efforts to get things right, can be highly imperfect and take a long time.

• • • • • • • •

If this book sparks your imagination for what's possible, then I have done my job. For it is upon Societal GRIT that the future of our species depends. Never has humankind, within and beyond its political boundaries, faced such daunting challenges and threats, nor such profound opportunities. All of these have three elements in common. They are complex, difficult, and protracted. They require immense and prolonged tenacity, resilience, and resolve. They also require hope and best efforts long after others have given in, or given up.

The darkest passages of human history have all shared the common poison of Strong, Bad, and Smart GRIT. When people and their armies amass and relentlessly set about to wreak severe and intentional harm, in ingenious ways, the cost of slowing, halting, and ideally preventing such efforts can be immense. Even the best-intentioned good can rank among the most devastating bad. When the Catholic missionaries set forth to "save," to bring God and enlightenment to the ignorant natives of the New World, one could argue (and hope), in the context of their society and times, their intentions were of the grandest good. The plague, enslavement, and devastation that resulted were clearly of the broadest bad.

While it's important to decode and confront the catastrophic power the wrong brand of Societal GRIT can unleash, it's far more energizing and constructive to explore the boundless upside the right brand of Societal GRIT can spawn. Take any challenge, no matter how great, and imagine, when enough of us employ Strong, Good, and Smart GRIT toward its resolution, how much greater our chances of surmounting, if not harnessing that challenge become. Sometimes it's just one person's vision that creates a ripple of Good, Smart, Strong GRIT all the way up the ladder.

When the global economic crisis struck, it took mere days for companies, industries, and societies to plummet into the abyss. But over the course of many years of austerity, and through lots of highly imperfect stops and starts, we witnessed most major economies gain firm footing on their path to recovery. The recovery was largely a patchwork of countries and collectives demonstrating varying degrees and inconsistent quality of GRIT.

This raises two points. First, notice that, despite all the significant imperfections—the less-than-Optimal GRIT—there was enough GRIT from enough societies and their leaders to work our way through. Optimal GRIT is rare and often exists as merely an aspiration or ideal. Second, imagine how much quicker and more completely we could have recovered, and how much real suffering could have been eliminated had there been more Optimal Societal GRIT, on both local and global scale.

Across Europe, where significant and prolonged sacrifice has been required, imagine if instead of the required *few*, the involved and affected *many* had stepped up personally and collectively, to dig deep, do whatever it takes to not only get past, but also to emerge stronger because of the crisis. The same question can be asked and principle applied to global climate change, a major epidemic, or any geopolitical adversity. In this sense, our collective GRIT determines our destiny. It is what decides whether ultimately we devolve or evolve. Over the course of my remaining years, if this book, this ever-evolving research and work, nudges the grand needle on Societal GRIT even a tick (and yes, I hope much more), I can think of no more meaningful result from my life's work.

Societal GRIT—Education

Consider the role of GRIT in education, as Angela Duckworth at Penn and her colleagues have brought to life. For most of the 20th century, the United States led the world in producing college graduates. But over the past twenty years, the U.S. has fallen from the top of those lists and is now ranked twelfth in the world in the percentage of young people who have earned a college degree. Incidentally, we are also twelfth in the world rankings on social well-being. Some would claim a relationship.

During those same decades, education has become more stratified, with more well-off students graduating at higher rates, while middle- and lower-class students struggle to complete a degree. Class, or one's station in life, seems to matter more than ever. But does it have to be that way?

We know GRIT matters. Not only is GRIT predictive of academic performance among disadvantaged and/or minority populations, it can also determine where you go in life.

In an independent study my team and I conducted in conjunction with a senior psychometrician at the Educational Testing Service, we discovered that GRIT is predictive of one's ability to rise up, to improve one's station in life over time. Those who score lower on GRIT tend to sag or stagnate. Those who score higher gain a meaningful advantage.

Imagine these sorts of gains on a mass scale. This is why applying GRIT, even in its most basic form (grit), to education has become one of my most pressing missions. Elevating society is a worthy quest.

"Kids with more grit are more likely to succeed."

**— ANGELA LEE DUCKWORTH, PSYCHOLOGIST,
ASSOCIATE PROFESSOR AT THE UNIVERSITY OF PENNSYLVANIA,
FOUNDER OF THE DUCKWORTH LAB**

LEADERSHIP GRIT

When it comes to GRIT and its consequences, leaders are the grand influencers and the great multipliers. In this way, they shape our course and history. Take this challenge: Knowing what you now know about GRIT, who is the grittiest leader you've ever known, or at least heard of? What was it about him or her that earned your pick? Or try this angle: Of anyone you've ever encountered, who showed the strongest, "goodest," and smartest GRIT? I'm going to make a wild guess that whomever you picked was/is, in fact, a leader, whether or not that person set out to be one. GRIT has the power to transcend formal title and make leaders out of men and women from even the most unlikely circumstances.

But it's not enough for a leader to have grit. He or she must have GRIT. As most of the amazing, gritty leaders I've researched, met, and written about in this book will tell you, there is a huge difference between a leader's being admired, and your feeling inspired. Leaders tend to spark a range of responses and perceptions, not all of them good. For example, a leader with Strong, but Dumb and/or Bad GRIT can destroy an organization. I've watched it happen.

I was working with one of the largest, hottest tech companies. Their stock was skyrocketing as they gobbled up market share as fast as the Internet could expand. The board decided to bring in a rock star CEO. He was charismatic, gritty, and tough. He also had a massive ego and was clearly more concerned about looking good in the press and pleasing external stakeholders than he was about his own people and products.

The market turned, and their stock began to cool. So, rather than rerouting, he got madder, more determined, and more forceful. He had set a path, announced it to "the Street," and was not about to back down. When his most seasoned global VP risked his career by raising his hand at a leadership retreat, asking, "Excuse me, but it's pretty clear our strategy is not working. We're getting killed. Isn't this the time for us to revisit our goals, or at least how we're going to achieve them?" A murmur of assent permeated the room.

The CEO paused, jumped to his feet, slammed the table with his fist, and all but screamed, "We do *not* quit! We do *not* give up! *Got* it?! If there's *one* thing I want you to know, damn it, it's this," he declared spittingly. "If what we are doing is not working, then try goddamned *harder! We set* the damn goals. We *have* the damn plan. Now go make the damn thing *happen!"*

The company has since gone out of business, for which the CEO got paid tens of millions of dollars in exit bonuses, and the result of which drained billions of dollars from millions of shareholders. Smart. Good. Strong. You need all three to be a gritty Leader.

Contrast this example with Elon Musk, founder and CEO of SpaceX. His vision to populate Mars with 1 million people, in order to help preserve the human race, isn't exactly modest, or in many experts' opinions, the least bit doable. But Musk thrives on taking on the long-term, seemingly impossible, most daunting, and compelling goals. This can take a toll on his people, while elevating them to greater heights than they could ever otherwise achieve. This means embracing bigger failures to achieve bigger wins.

According to Dolly Singh, who worked for Musk for five years as the former head of talent acquisition for SpaceX, the moment their Falcon 1 rocket failed and was propelled uncontrollably into outer space, Elon Musk showed what GRITty leadership is all about.

"When Elon came out he walked past the press and first addressed the company. Although his exact words escape me in how he started off, the essence of his comments were that:

- We knew this was going to be hard; it is after all rocket science. Then he listed the half dozen or so countries that had failed to even successfully execute a first-stage flight and get to outer space, a feat we had accomplished successfully that day.

- Elon has (in his infinite wisdom) prepared for the possibility of an issue with the flight by taking on a significant investment (from Draper Fisher Jurvetson, if I recall correctly), providing SpaceX with ample financial resources to attempt two more launches, and giving us security until at least flight five, if needed.

- And that we need to pick ourselves up and dust ourselves off, because we have a lot of work to do. Then he said, with as much fortitude and ferocity as he could muster after having been awake for like twenty-plus hours by this point, 'For my part, I will never give up and I mean never,' and that if we stick with him, we will win.

"I think most of us would have followed him into the gates of hell carrying suntan oil after that. It was the most impressive display of leadership that I have ever witnessed. Within moments, the energy of the building went from despair and defeat to a massive buzz of determination as people began to focus on moving forward instead of looking back. This shift happened collectively, across all 300-plus people in a matter of not more than five seconds. I wish I had video footage as I would love to analyze the shifts in body language that occurred over those five seconds. It was an unbelievably powerful experience."

Musk is known for giving his people brutally tough feedback, and having insanely high expectations, to the point, according to Singh, that people feel they are "staring into the abyss." And that sets an overtly gritty cultural tone. "We were very honest with people that when you join SpaceX you are choosing a thorny path; and we sort of expect you to enjoy, honor, and appreciate that opportunity," Singh says. "This may sound harsh, but you don't get to Mars … with a bunch of softies."

In one of my recent books, *The Adversity Advantage*, I teamed up with Erik Weihenmayer, the first blind person to ascend Everest and the Seven Summits, among countless other breathtaking feats. Beyond his tremendous character, I wrote about and partnered with Erik due in large part to his exceptional resilience, his Adversity Quotient®. He literally scores off the charts and is an exemplar of what I teach. But I mention Erik again briefly here because of his evolution from a gritty guy to a gritty *leader*.

How completely understandable would it have been for Erik to stand on the summit of Everest in 2001 and holler to the heavens, "I did it!" How understandable would it be for a blind guy to milk that moment for the rest of his life? Instead, Erik used the summit of Everest and the Seven Summits of the world as his base camp for a much grittier, lifelong ascent.

He evolved *his* aspirations to more fully leverage his personal GRIT and story, in order to inspire and awaken others to elevate *their* aspirations for the contribution they can make to help them pioneer new possibilities in their lives. Although the exact words were different, Erik sat back and asked himself his version of the Leadership GRIT question: "How can I leverage myself to have the greatest positive impact on others, creating an organization that infuses others with the GRIT it takes to make their boldest aspirations come true?"

In addition to sharing his message by speaking to tens of thousands of people per year, and being an inspirational exemplar of what he preaches by taking on adventures like whitewater kayaking the Colorado River (solo kayak!) with his gritty support team, Erik created and funded the gritty organization No Barriers. He seeks not only to reach, but also to help truly gritify more people. The No Barriers motto is simple: "What's within you is stronger than what's in your way." Gritty leaders set gritty goals, grow gritty people, and create the real breakthroughs that advance us all.

Gritty Business

As a customer or client, what do you value most? Quality? Speed? Dependability? Design? Brand? Service? Reputation? All of these and any other paragons of value all share one thing in common. They're tough. *Really tough.* Delivering any of these once or occasionally is one thing; delivering these at top levels—reliably, flawlessly, and consistently—puts you at the top. People pay for what they value and customers and clients pay more for those things that have been produced with the greatest GRIT.

GRIT Challenge—GRITTY SERVICE

As Cary Pappas, president and CEO of FedEx TechConnect, will tell you, "FedEx was built on speed, reliability, and quality services. Because of that foundation, our customers have come to expect perfection. To make it all possible, our Customer Service team works day in and day out to help quickly resolve any issues our customers may have with their shipments. Of course unexpected obstacles arise, but relying on their grit, our team is always determined to overcome any challenges they may face. After leading this Customer Service team for over twelve years, I can say with confidence that they bring a positive attitude and can-do spirit to any situation they may encounter. And that same grit is driving our performance to new heights."

* * *

It's not always easy to spot GRIT. It hides beneath the calmest, often most polished exteriors. Walk into the serene, floral-scented sanctuary of Ron's Nursery in the sleepy little working-class town of Grover Beach and, frankly, GRIT is about the last thing on your mind. And that's exactly the way Ron Carlock, its gregarious founder, wants it. It takes about four seconds to recognize the incredible passion, detail, and eye for delight Ron pours into every nook and cranny of his shop. You can travel to the finest shops in the country, and beyond, and find yourself asking, "Isn't that the same one Ron sells?"

"Hey great place!" "Wow, you sure do a beautiful job here!" Those are the comments from a couple of customers as I wait to chat with the man himself. What those customers don't see is the GRIT. Ron poured everything he had into building his dream. It took years, decades to build, but he dug deep to design, decorate, fill, and launch something folks around here had never seen. It was the flagship nursery and home decoration store for the entire region. He had acres of plants, waterfalls, and pathways, along with the highest-end soaps, candles, planters, furniture, and so much more. People came from far and wide to just tour, or experience "Ron's." It wasn't a shop; it was a destination.

Then the Great Recession hit. And the luxury goods market, especially locally, got gutted. Ron was brought to his knees. But Ron's got G-R-I-T. It pours out in every word and decision. Ron constantly seeks new ideas, input, and approaches. He literally used this adversity to reinvent himself and his business. He rerouted rather than fold. And he refused to give up, when almost anyone else would.

Essentially broke, he rented a much smaller space, which he initially decorated pretty sparsely, using what little money he had. This time he scanned the planet even more intensely, knowing he had to bring in fresh ideas, perspectives, products, and displays. Along the way, he paid careful attention to how people responded to some of his innovative approaches.

A lot of stuff he brought in, like materials made out of painted, recycled oil drums, people were seeing for the first time. Based on the feedback he voraciously sought, he continually refined, tweaked, and adjusted his approach. It was touch and go for a long time. But over time, week by week, he rebuilt the scaled-down but equally wonderful and vibrant Ron's. And at age sixty-four, he's in there every day, delighting his customers with his newest inventions and creations. Sometimes you have to wade through the muck to enjoy beauty on the other side.

●　■　■　■　▾　■　●

Nick Lowinger is sixteen. At five years old, he visited a homeless shelter and remembers being sad that the kids there didn't have good shoes; some had no shoes. He became dedicated to solving this situation and by twelve years old, started the Gotta Have Sole Foundation. What began as a dream was created as a community service project and now has gone nationwide.

To date, Nick has donated more than 20,000 pairs of new shoes to homeless children throughout the United States. His new organization, SOLEdiers, donates shoes to homeless military veterans and their families. You don't need a Harvard MBA or even a high school diploma to use your GRIT to grow a gritty business and to do good in the world.

> *"If you decide that you're going to do only the things you know are going to work, you're going to leave a lot of opportunity on the table."*
> — JEFF BEZOS, FOUNDER AND CEO OF AMAZON.COM

The same gritty business principles play out on the global scale. You may never have heard of or seen the Fisker Karma. There's a reason. It was a high-end, stunning hybrid luxury sports car, designed by Henrik Fisker of BMW and Aston Martin fame. And for a while, it was all the buzz among motor enthusiasts. It was going to upend the luxury and hybrid markets, disrupt the sports car world, and more. Given its immense promise and "green" credentials, Fisker even received $500 million in funding from the United States government, an investment that later became one of the embarrassments of the Obama administration.

I attended one of the first investor meetings ever held, at the Fisker headquarters in Orange County, California. As soon as I heard Fisker's and his top executives' presentations, I turned to my colleague and said, "These guys are doomed." I pulled my investment and ran. And it wasn't because they didn't know their stuff, or have the capability to produce a great car. It's just that GRIT is a powerful lens. Instead of hearing the smartest, best versions of Growth, Resilience, Instinct, and Tenacity, I heard arrogance and a decent dose of Dumb GRIT. What they were striving for, how they were anticipating and attacking obstacles, and how they were going after their goals left me highly unimpressed.

Contrast that with Tesla. Tesla, founded by CEO Elon Musk, has essentially accomplished everything Fisker failed to do, and more. It has achieved brand superiority by pioneering the near impossible. Any seasoned business leader will tell you that creating a new brand of automobile is one of the toughest quests anyone can embark upon. It takes years, if not decades to navigate the gauntlet of lobbyists, regulations, and immense costs, not to mention getting customers to plop down $75,000 for a car they've never heard of, and that can't promise to be around when you need repairs.

Elon Musk is an exemplar of GRIT. He doesn't set out to make a product. Whether it's Tesla, SpaceX, SolarCity, or Hyperloop, a new concept for high-speed mass transit, he sets out with an interplanetary perspective to fix a problem in a way that benefits humanity, our planet, i.e., *any others*. He doesn't let obstacles like relatively weak, extremely expensive electric batteries with a limited lifespan hold him back. Instead you can imagine him asking, "What if we teamed up with other leading companies and reinvented the electric battery in a way that improves not just our cars, but also the world?" And that is exactly what he's doing.

Two bright leaders, two companies competing for the same market, both with tremendous expertise and credibility. The one with true GRIT, the "Goodest," Smartest, and Strongest GRIT, prevails.

Imagine a beach and that experience of sinking your toes in the sand—or the wear and tear of running in that same sand and forming a blister on untrained bare feet—which is created by the accumulation of a lot of almost microscopic granules. The same thing is true of a gritty business. It is built on the granules of gritty goal by gritty goal (see **Grow—Advanced**), gritty decision by gritty decision, and gritty effort by gritty effort.

As a customer, with which company would you rather do business? The one that takes the easy path, does the bare minimum, and tends to crumble when the going gets too rough? Or the one that sets bold, gritty, maybe pioneering goals on design, quality, service, brand, capability, features, and more, then digs deep and does whatever it takes to make it happen, over and over again? GRIT is the engine of exceptional shareholder and market value, sustainable competitive edge, and creating the kind of brand that talent and customers flock to, even in adverse economic conditions.

GRITTY EDUCATION

Launch is the highly selective four-week summer entrepreneurship program held at MIT, created and led by Laurie Stach. Not only do I have the privilege of teaching GRIT to these exceptional students twice each summer, Laurie also uses our assessment in their screening process. Of course, the students are off-the-charts bright. That's a given.

The whole experience is super intense. They essentially form then compete in teams over four weeks to go from concept to a minimal viable product (MVP), which they pitch to angel investors for actual funding. Over the first week or two, fatigue and stress take their toll, and it grows from there. As you might guess, it's not necessarily the teams with the most promising ideas, but the teams who show the greatest GRIT that generally prevail. It is literally predictive of their success.

The Launch experience raises an important issue. Even if your team demonstrates a reasonable level of Growth, Resilience, Instinct, and Tenacity, the question becomes, "At what price?" In other words, how Robust is your team? How well does it hold up, even thrive under the chronic stress and demands placed upon it? Robustness is key. And within any team the quality is as important (and often more important) than the quantity of GRIT.

A 9 percent increase in GRIT in just four months.

Scott Swaaley, Director, GRITLab, High Tech High, San Diego, California

GRITLab: "Where Skillset Meets Mindset."

Imagine growing greater GRIT in students. To see if it were possible, I teamed up with national award-winning teacher Scott Swaaley on his pioneering GRITLab project at High Tech High School, a forward-thinking San Diego-based charter school focusing on project-based learning. Scott was so inspired by their approach, he left his high-paying gig as an electrical engineer and renewable energy consultant to become a ninth-grade physics teacher and see what impact he could have on young people's lives.

High Tech High's project room.

Scott Swaaley's classroom at High Tech High. The evolution of the design through multiple prototypes.

Scott was convinced traditional education was pretty broken, and since he's not afraid to invent new approaches, the GRITLab was born.

"Adversity Scaffolding," or "Adversity by Design," is the term we use for the method he employs to jolt and keep his students out of their comfort zone. It is through the combination of GRIT-based lessons and tools, along with the increasing levels of frustration and struggles built into each project, that Scott's students grow measurably greater GRIT. In Round One, we saw a 9 percent overall improvement of GRIT. I suspect, given Scott's GRIT, the next round will be even stronger.

Scott has been awarded for his innovative approach to education by the Paul G. Allen Family Foundation, San Diego Foundation, Aerospace Physiology Society, McGraw-Hill, MIT InvenTeams, the Teaching Channel, and two documentaries, currently in post-production.

Thanks to the pioneering vision and efforts of Brian Tietje, vice provost at California Polytechnic State University, and Amy Baldwin, director of University College at University of Central Arkansas, as well as our partnership with learning company Pearson, GRIT is being introduced on the front end of college life through Pearson's series of advice- and insight-packed publications under the title *The College Experience*. Gaining GRIT early in the journey, ideally at the very beginning, equips students to make better, grittier choices and dig deeper to enhance their chances of fulfilling gritty goals. With GRIT, they can "get in, get through, get out, and get paid," which is the promise upon which Tietje and Baldwin built their leading authority on the subject.

GRITTY INNOVATION

Creativity is inherently an exercise in hope. You have to believe something that does not exist can. Innovation—turning the idea into something real—is, however, an exercise of GRIT. This is where the difference between grit 1.0 and GRIT 2.0 becomes particularly pronounced.

Magdalena G. Grohman, the associate director of the Center for Value in Medicine, Science and Technology at the University of Texas at Dallas, argues that grittiness is not the end-all, be-all for student success. "When you look at it, these (the areas studied by Dr. Angela Duckworth) are well-defined areas and the rules for achievement are well defined in those areas," she explains. "We know what to do to get good grades, what to do to stay in military school, and what to do to win in contests such as spelling bees … But what about creative achievement?" In two separate analyses, Grohman found basic grit was not predictive of students' creative achievements and endeavors, including visual and performing arts, writing, scientific ingenuity, or even creative problem solving.

Even when you take into account the perspective of one's peers and teachers, the grit-creativity link may appear weak. In a separate study at Yale University's Center for Emotional Intelligence, those students rated highest on creativity were not necessarily those rated highest on basic grit. However, students' ratings of openness to new experiences (Growth dimension of GRIT) and passion for their work (Tenacity) did predict creativity. So, with basic grit, the results are mixed.

On the other hand, it is my consistent observation that while grit doesn't predict innovation, GRIT does. For students at all levels, entrepreneurs like Ron Carlock or Elon Musk, or anyone trying to get from here to there, the capacity to not just keep trying and persisting (basic grit), but also to demonstrate full G-R-I-T is what makes the difference. Combining Growth (seeking new, fresh, perspectives, input, approaches); Resilience (responding optimally to whatever adversity comes your way); Instinct (reassessing, refining, and rerouting as needed); and Tenacity (applying all the rest—G-R-I—to relentlessly pursue that goal or solve that problem) is the very essence of innovation.

> **For anyone trying to get from here to there, the capacity to not just keep trying and persisting (basic grit) but also to demonstrate full G-R-I-T is what makes the difference.**

I think Magdalena Grohman is right: basic grit, by itself, may not cut it. But I've discovered there's a reason why the lead innovators at some of the top companies in the world, as well as the more than 100,000 entrepreneurs with whom I've had the privilege to work (many who defined their industries), never tire of measuring and improving their GRIT. Bringing an idea to fruition, generating real innovation, is its very essence.

OPTIMAL GRIT

It's simple. But like almost anything worth achieving, it's tough. Demonstrating Strong, Good, and Smart G-R-I-T (Growth, Resilience, Instinct, and Tenacity), drawing from all four capacities (Emotional, Mental, Physical, Spiritual), across all situations, and ascending all the rungs (Individual, Relational, Team, Organizational, Societal) is the surest path to an optimal career and life. You will fortify your path toward Optimal GRIT by continuing what you've begun and completing the remaining Advanced portions of this book: Gauge and Grow.

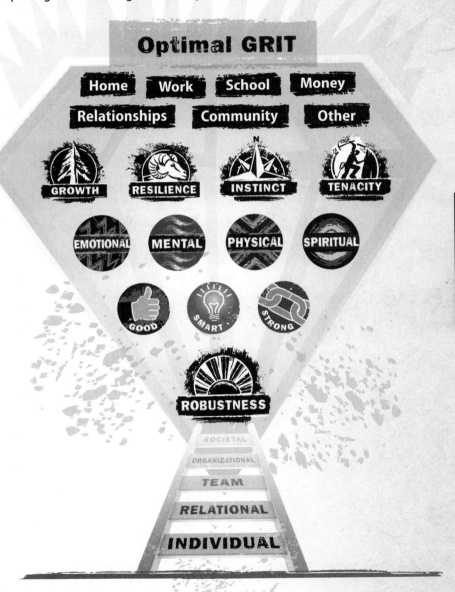

Are you ready to peel back the layers and go deeper into your GRIT? That is the purpose of this section. As you do—as you take on and explore your personal GRIT Mix—you will discover that you are now, after reading this far, more aware, more effective, and more deliberate in your efforts to build and show GRIT. Customize your journey through the GRIT Mix. Attack it however it most benefits you.

The GRIT Mix Challenge

As you embark on this next stage of *GRIT,* this point is worth repeating: GRIT is everywhere, in everyone. The GRIT Challenge served up in the opening of this book—putting on my GRIT Lens and literally going outside, exploring my town, and uncovering everyday stories—really brought it home for me, and I hope for you too: how GRIT *is* the story and oxygen of achievement.

It's not some rare, mythic quality reserved for legendary heroes. It is the required fuel of everyday endeavors, everyday life. And it is what gives you or anyone a real shot at having life become a bit more extraordinary and abundant than it otherwise would be. You now know it's not a matter of if you do or don't have it. It's about *how much* and *what kinds* of GRIT you have and use. It's about your GRIT Mix.

Your GRIT Mix Journal

As my team and I tested the GRIT Mix on others, it became readily apparent how important and useful it was for people to write stuff down. You'll want to capture your responses, really pause and reflect, even compare your future, more gritified self against the one you capture with your GRIT Mix today. For that reason, we've created the GRIT Mix Journal. You can access a complimentary copy at www.gritgauge.com. Or you can simply make your own. Whatever serves the purpose of having you fully engage in Gauging your own GRIT.

Tips

Engage Intensely

Intensity trumps time. This section deserves your finest effort. You intuitively know what science has now proved: The more intensely you engage in this process of self-reflection, the more it will stick. The science says the intensity of your focus and effort radically influences how much and how quickly you "myelinate" or hardwire both lessons and habits. Putting that science to practice is pretty simple. Give it your best as you pause, discuss, and/or jot down your answers to the questions throughout the GRIT Mix Challenge. Some people prefer to create a journal to document their journey or simply as a portable tool for reflection.

Seek Input from Others

Many of these provocations require the kind of insight that you may want others to help provide, by simply turning or reaching out to the right person/people and asking, "How would *you* answer this one?" Even if it's inconvenient, it's worth asking. We all have blind spots. The more honest, external input you solicit, the more of the full picture you're likely to paint.

Focus and Be Honest

Based on experience doing and teaching this, the GRIT Mix requires not just your uncompromised focus and effort, but also your unvarnished *honesty*. I guess you could say it takes some GRIT to get the most out of *GRIT!* You'll want to tap your Smart GRIT. Short concentrated bursts with full engagement are better and far more effective than long stretches of halfhearted involvement.

Let's begin by turning the model of the GRIT Grid Cube into a tool. We'll disassemble it (three continua and six sides), so you can take a hard look at your GRIT from every angle. You can then reassemble the pieces to get a holographic view of your current and potential GRIT. You may choose to tap your GRIT Gauge report to inform some of your answers.

THE GRIT GRID CUBE

Before you knew much about the real theory and science of GRIT, if someone had simply asked you, "On a scale of 1–10, compared to everyone else, how much grit do you have?" what would you have said? How would you have scored your basic, everyday grit?

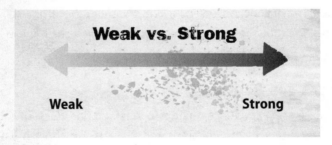

Place a bold "**X**" on the continuum above to honestly represent your overall level or strength of GRIT.

Now that you know what you know, on a scale of 1–10 (10 is strongest possible), compared to everyone else, how strong or weak is your GRIT? I'm not talking about in different moments or situations, or certain capacities, but *overall*. If a ten is the person with the strongest imaginable GRIT, and one is essentially the one with nearly none, where do you rank? If you can, go ahead and jot down your number on the continua arrow above.

Now go deeper.

```
Sample Section of GRIT MIX JOURNAL

WEAK ←——————————→ STRONG

My GRIT — Historically

STRONG _____
_____
_____

WEAK _____
_____
_____

Current

GRIT FLUX _____
_____
_____

SITUATION/CONTEXT _____
_____
_____
```

To begin, consider your history. As you think back on your life, even your recent months or days:

1. *Stronger*—In what specific ways and in what specific instances have you shown the greatest (strongest) GRIT?
   - What effect did it have? What, if any, consequences (good or bad) did it create?
   - How did others react? What effect did your GRIT have on the people around you?

2. *Weaker*—In what specific instances could, or even should you have shown more or stronger GRIT? Where/when, on what dimension, was your GRIT relatively the weakest?
   - What effect did your less-than-optimal GRIT have?

- What happened? What *didn't* happen?
- If you had demonstrated greater GRIT, how do you think things would have turned out differently? What effect would it likely have had?

Now, shift your perspective from history to present day.

3. **GRIT Flux**—All of us have some flux or variation in our GRIT. Some show extremely strong GRIT in some situations and extremely weak GRIT in others. Other people have very consistent GRIT.

On the continuum shown below, how much does your GRIT tend to vary or fluctuate, moment to moment, situation by situation, and day by day?

Assuming there are some differences, what are the two to three most important factors that influence your GRIT flux and how much it goes up and down? What can catapult you to a ten? What demotivates you to a three?
- If it were to vary less and be more consistent, specifically how do you think that might affect you? Others? Those around you? What, if any, benefits might it bring?

4. **Context, Strongest Situational GRIT**—In what situations or context(s) do you tend to show the most or strongest GRIT? (Friends, family, work, school, community, hobbies, by yourself, etc.)
- Why do you show more GRIT there?
- What are the contributing factors?
- As you bring your relatively high GRIT, what are the upsides and/or downsides for you? Others?
- What, if any, key examples come to mind?

5. **Context, Weakest Situational GRIT**—In what situations or context(s) do you tend to show the least or weakest GRIT? (Friends, family, work, school, community, hobbies, by yourself, etc.)

- Why do you show less GRIT there?
- What are the contributing factors?
- When you show relatively weaker GRIT, what are the upsides and/or downsides for you? Others? For example, does it make other people want to help you? Does it make them feel closer to you in some way?
- What, if any, key examples come to mind?

6. *Context, Strongest Rungs of GRIT*—For which rungs in the GRIT Ladder do you comparatively tend to show the most or strongest GRIT? (Individual, Relational, Team, Organizational, Societal.)
   - How would those who know you best answer this question?
   - Why do you show more GRIT there?
   - What are the contributing factors?
   - What are the benefits/consequences to you and others as you show your level-specific, relatively strongest GRIT?
   - What, if any, important examples come to mind?

7. *Context, Weakest Rungs of GRIT*—For which rungs in the GRIT Ladder do you comparatively tend to show the least or weakest GRIT? (Individual, Relational, Team, Organizational, Societal.)
   - How would those who know you best answer this question?
   - Why do you show less GRIT there?
   - What factors have the biggest effect on how much you show?
   - As you show relatively less GRIT at that level, what are the positives and/or negatives for you? Others?
   - What would be one or two rich examples?

8. *Context, Strongest Capacity of GRIT*—Of the four GRIT capacities (Emotional, Mental, Physical, Spiritual), which one is your strongest?
   - Think about the people who know you better than anyone else. How would they answer this question?
   - Why is that specific capacity your strongest?
   - What are the best and worst consequences as you put that capacity into play? For you? Others? For example, if it is Physical, does it make others see you as strong, someone they can count on to endure, to work, to handle the physically demanding tasks?
   - What would be the most important one or two examples?

9. **Context, Weakest Capacity of GRIT**—Of the four GRIT capacities (Emotional, Mental, Physical, Spiritual), which one is your weakest?
   - How would those who know you best answer this question?
   - Why is that specific capacity your weakest?
   - What factors contribute to its being your weakest?
   - What are the upsides and/or downsides of this being your weakest capacity, for you? Others? For example, if it is Emotional, does it make others protect you from bad news? Does it give you more permission to get upset?
   - What, if any, key examples come to mind?

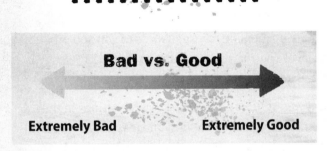

Place a bold "**X**" on the continuum above to represent your net, actual blend of Bad to Good GRIT.

Everyone demonstrates some mix of both Good and Bad GRIT. Remember, Good GRIT is defined by relentlessly pursuing things that are ultimately beneficial to you and (ideally) others, and Bad GRIT is the opposite. It means pursuing stuff that even unintentionally is damaging or harmful to yourself or others. Again, the key phrase is "even unintentionally." Much of Bad GRIT is unintentional.

Given these definitions:

1. *Good*—On the Bad to Good Continuum (above), where do you land? How Good do you think your *overall* GRIT tends to be in comparison to everyone else?

2. *Bad*—What proportion of the goals that you pursue
   - Honestly end up being a "net positive," benefiting others?
   - Benefit you more than, or even at the expense of, others?
   - Have little, if any, real benefit?
   - End up being a "net negative" to others, causing more downside than upside (even unintentionally)?

- Are intentionally or unintentionally, over time, more damaging to others than to you?
- Start out with good intentions, but end with bad results?
- Examples that come to mind?

3. *Good/How*—In what specific ways do you (or have you) recently shown the "goodest" or best GRIT?
   - How did (or does) that affect you? Others?
   - How did (or does) it make you feel?

4. *Bad/How*—In what specific ways do you demonstrate Bad, or your worst version of GRIT?
   - What effect did (or does) demonstrating your worst version of GRIT have on you? Others?
   - How did (or does) it make you feel?

5. *Bad to Good GRIT Flux*—Beyond your Bad to Good overall Mix, how much does your Bad to Good GRIT vary? Based on the Bad to Good Continuum ("Extremely Bad" to "Extremely Good"), how much does your GRIT fluctuate from bad to good, moment to moment, situation by situation, and day by day?
   - How bad is your worst, and how good is your best?
   - If you had to put markers on the continuum, what's your full range?

- Is your fluctuation extreme, modest, or minimal?
- Assuming, like most people, there are some differences, why do you think your GRIT varies?
- What are the two to three most potent factors that influence the degree and direction of your GRIT, from good to bad?
- If your GRIT were to fluctuate less dramatically and become more consistently Good, specifically how do you think that might affect you? Others? What, if any, benefits might it bring?

6A. *Context, "Goodest" Situational GRIT*— In what situations or context(s) do you tend to show the best or "goodest" GRIT? (Friends, family, work, school, community, hobbies, by yourself, etc.)
- Why do you show more Good GRIT there?
- What are the key contributing factors?
- How does showing your "goodest" GRIT in this situation affect you? Others?

6B. *Context, "Baddest" Situational GRIT*—In what situations or context(s) do you tend to show the worst or "baddest" GRIT? (Friends, family, work, school, community, hobbies, by yourself, etc.)
- Why do you show more Bad GRIT there?
- What factors contribute the most to that happening?
- When you show your "baddest" GRIT in that situation, how does that affect you? Others?

> *Everyone* demonstrates some mix of both Good and Bad GRIT. **Good GRIT** is relentlessly pursuing things that are ultimately beneficial to you and (ideally) others. **Bad GRIT** is the opposite.

7A. *Context, "Goodest" Rungs of GRIT*—At what rung(s) of the GRIT Ladder do you comparatively tend to show your best or most beneficial GRIT? (Individual, Relational, Team, Organizational, Societal)
- Why do you think that you show more Good GRIT there?
- What factors have the biggest influence on how Good your GRIT is at that rung or level?
- When you show Good GRIT at that rung, how does that affect you? Others?
- What, if any, key examples come to mind?

7B. *Context, "Baddest" Rungs of GRIT*—At what rung(s) of the GRIT Ladder do you comparatively tend to show your worst or most damaging GRIT? (Individual, Relational, Team, Organizational, Societal)
- Why do you show your worst GRIT there?
- What are the contributing factors?

- What effect does it have on you, others, when you show your worst GRIT at that rung?
- When/where has that occurred?
- How would improving this help?

8A. *Context, "Goodest" Capacity of GRIT*—Of the four GRIT capacities (Emotional, Mental, Physical, Spiritual), which one shows your best and contributes the most benefit?
- Why and how is that your "Goodest" capacity?
- What factors have the biggest influence on how much of that capacity you show?
- How does it typically come out or show up?
- When you use or flex that capacity, how does that affect you? Others?
- When, where, and how has that happened in the past?

For example, some people use their Spiritual GRIT to get others to experience hope in an otherwise hopeless situation.

8B. *Context, "Baddest" Capacity of GRIT*—Of the four GRIT capacities (Emotional, Mental, Physical, Spiritual), which one brings out your worst GRIT or is the most potentially damaging?
- Why and how is that capacity your worst/most damaging?
- What are the key contributing factors?
- How does that capacity typically come out or show up?
- When you use or flex that capacity, how does that affect you? Others?
- What, if any, key examples come to mind?

For example, some people use their Physical GRIT to the point of injury, or even pushing others beyond their capabilities.

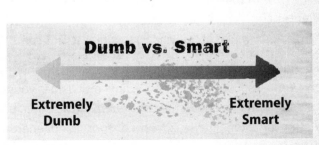

Dumb vs. Smart

Extremely Dumb ←——————————→ **Extremely Smart**

Place a bold **"X"** on the continuum above to represent your net, actual blend of Dumb to Smart GRIT.

Pretty much everyone also shows a personal blend of Smart and Dumb GRIT. If Dumb GRIT is defined by relentlessly pursuing less-than-optimal goals in less-than-optimal ways, and Smart GRIT is the inverse (pursuing the most important things in the best or most optimal ways), think about how others would describe your blend.

1. *Smart*—If you had to pick a spot on the Dumb to Smart continuum, what's your GRIT Mix? How Smart do you think your *overall* GRIT tends to be, in comparison to everyone else?

2. *Dumb*—What proportion of the goals that you pursue:
   • Is absolutely, without question, the best thing for you to pursue?
   • Is pursued in the best possible—most efficient and effective—way?
   • Is clearly a poor use of your energy, effort, and/or time?
   • Could be pursued in smarter—more efficient and effective—ways?

3. *Smart/How*—In what specific ways do you, or have you recently shown the smartest GRIT?
   • When you showed your smartest GRIT, what effect did that have on you? On others?
   • How did it make you feel when you showed your smartest GRIT?
   • What, if any, key examples of your smartest GRIT come to mind?

4. *Dumb/How*—In what specific ways have you demonstrated your dumbest version of GRIT?
   • When you did, what effect did (or does) that have on you? Others?
   • How did (or does) it make you feel when you show your dumbest GRIT?
   • Is there any pattern to where or how you demonstrate dumber vs. smarter GRIT?
   • What, if any, key examples of showing your dumbest GRIT come to mind?

5. *Dumb to Smart GRIT Flux*—Using the Dumb to Smart Continuum ("Extremely Dumb" to "Extremely Smart"), how much does your GRIT vary or fluctuate from one end of the continuum to the other, based on the situation, time (of day, week, year), or your mood (energy, mindset, etc.)?
   • If you had to put markers on the continuum, what's your full range?
   • In your opinion, is your fluctuation extreme, modest, or minimal?

Dumb to Smart GRIT Flux

No Variation ←→ **Extreme Variation**

- Assuming, like most people, there are some differences, why do you think your GRIT varies as much as it does?
- What are the two to three most potent factors that influence the degree and nature of your GRIT, from dumber to smarter?
- If your GRIT were to fluctuate less dramatically and become more consistently Smart, specifically how do you think that might affect you? Others? What, if any, benefits would you imagine it might create?

6A. *Context, Smartest Situational GRIT*—In what situations or context(s) do you tend to show your smartest GRIT? (Friends, family, work, school, community, hobbies, by yourself, etc.)
- Why do you think that you show smarter GRIT there?
- What factors play the biggest role?
- What examples of showing your smartest GRIT in that context come to mind?
- When you show your smartest GRIT, how does this affect you? Others?

6B. *Context, Dumbest Situational GRIT*—In what situations or context(s) do you tend to show your dumbest GRIT? (Friends, family, work, school, community, hobbies, by yourself, etc.)
- Why do you show dumber GRIT there?
- What factors play the biggest role in sparking your dumbest GRIT?
- What, if any, key examples come to mind?
- When you do, how does your showing relatively dumber GRIT affect you? Others?

7A. *Context, Smartest Rungs of GRIT*—At what rung(s) of the GRIT Ladder do you comparatively tend to show your smartest GRIT? (Individual, Relational, Team, Organizational, Societal)
- Why do you show smarter GRIT at that rung?
- What additional factors play the biggest role in that happening?
- When you do show smarter GRIT at that level, what, if any, upsides or downsides does that cause for you? Others?

GAUGE—ADVANCED

7B. **Context, Dumbest Rungs of GRIT**—At what rung(s) of the GRIT Ladder do you comparatively tend to show your dumbest GRIT? (Individual, Relational, Team, Organizational, Societal)
- Why do you show your relatively dumbest GRIT there?
- What are the key contributing factors in your showing your dumbest GRIT at that rung?
- When you do show relatively dumber GRIT at that level, how does this affect you? Others?

8A. **Context, Smartest Capacity of GRIT**—Which GRIT capacity (Emotional, Mental, Physical, Spiritual) do you tap the most to show your smartest GRIT?
- How does that show up or come out?
- How might or how does it tend to affect you, others, when you put it to use?
- What's an example from your life of how you used this capacity to show your smartest GRIT?
- What changes are you going to make?

For instance, someone might use Emotional GRIT to defuse an irate customer or boss, and accelerate the path to real solutions.

8B. **Context, Weakest Capacity of GRIT**—Which GRIT capacity (Emotional, Mental, Physical, Spiritual) do you tap the most to show your dumbest GRIT?
- How does that capacity show up or come out?
- How might or how does it tend to affect you, others, when you put that capacity to use?
- What's an example from your life of how you used this capacity to show your dumbest GRIT?

For instance, someone might use Mental GRIT to keep analyzing ways to solve a problem long after the issue is dead, and it's smarter to move on.

Robustness

I'd be doing you a real disservice if I didn't give you a chance to pause and ponder this culminating factor. As you've seen and no doubt experienced, exercising GRIT wears some people down, and it builds others up. Over the course of years and decades, some people fatigue and dim. Others fortify and brighten, staying fully alive until their final breath. That's our quest.

When you put together all the pieces (G-R-I-T, Strong/Weak, Good/Bad, Smart/Dumb, Emotional, Mental, Physical, Spiritual, at each rung of the GRIT Ladder), how has your GRIT journey affected you so far? How much wear and tear have you experienced along the way?

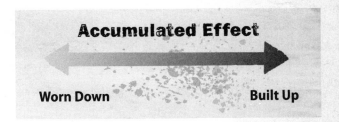

Accumulated Effect

Worn Down　　　　　　Built Up

Place a bold **"X"** on the continuum above to represent the accumulated effect life has had on you—your energy, optimism, effort, determination—so far.

- What ways have you held up relatively the best? (Mentally, physically, etc.)
- In what ways has life taken the relatively toughest toll on you? (Relationships, optimism, health, financial, etc.)
- If you could be significantly more robust—hold up better against and be more immune to whatever life throws your way—specifically how would that affect you? Those around you?
- What would you experience more or less of as a result?

GRIT Mix—REFLECTIONS

Now that you have successfully completed the GRIT Mix Challenge—forcing yourself, I hope, to confront, ponder, and answer the barrage of provocations I threw your way—here are some final reflections to pull it all together. As a result of your experience with the GRIT Mix Challenge,

- What was/is the biggest "aha!" or takeaway revelation for you?
- What are three to five additional key realizations?
- How do you feel about your current, overall GRIT Mix?
- What is the single biggest or most important adjustment you need to make? Where do you most need to improve?
- Overall, in what ways has your GRIT Mix served you best?
- Overall, in what ways has it hurt or hindered you?
- As you measurably strengthen your GRIT Mix and move along the path toward Optimal GRIT, in what specific ways do you most hope to benefit? Less what? More what?

As you take on the next, final section of the book, and as you apply the advanced tools, you should be able to make additional, meaningful strides on your path to Optimal GRIT.

"The bigger your challenges, the bigger your opportunity for growth."
– SWAMI VIVEKANANDA, INDIAN HINDU MONK

You will find this bonus section to be brief and, we hope, powerful. Each piece—each lesson and tool—is condensed to its bare essence, so you can apply it more readily.

You've navigated and wrestled through this entire book to get to this point. Unlike most readers who scan, peruse, and give up, you've stuck with it and are clearly serious about growing your GRIT even more. You've come to the right place. That's what these remaining pages are all about.

It's important for you to know that the three advanced-grade tools you're about to tackle come from not just the pristine ponds of scholarly research, but also from the muddy trenches of real people and real companies fighting to achieve real stuff, and in many cases, the most critical and gnarly stuff life can serve up.

Of the various GRIT Gainers we teach, I've selected these three as the most important to up your game (and GRIT).

Gritty Goals is a simple, quick tool to bolster and gritify any goal, with anyone, in any situation, at any rung or level.

The Gritty Game Plan is a way to gritify any strategy on how you are going to fulfill any gritty goal. It is used for everything from directing the efforts of multibillion-dollar global enterprises to a counselor working with a kid who's simply trying to graduate from school, and all the stuff in between.

The GRIT Gang is as much a provocation as a tool. It's designed to mess with your head and get you to rethink with whom you do and should surround yourself and, ideally, with whom you join up to make the big stuff happen.

These are adversity-tested, pressure-forged tools. They come from executives who've been up against the ropes or worn thin by the hailstorm of adversity that pelts them 24/7. These tools come from kids feeling lost, apathetic, unclear, or unequipped. They come from parents at their wits' end with how to de-wimpify their kids, or educators struggling to better position their students to succeed in a gritty world. They come from entrepreneurs scrapping to beat the odds, bring their innovations to life, and build a better world. And if you put them to good use, you can too.

"No GRIT, no pearl."
— ANONYMOUS

THE ROOTS OF SUCCESS

GRIT, represented by the roots that tenaciously and relentlessly reach out, both anchors you and fuels your growth. The solid, stable trunk is your Self—your unshakable character, values, and essence—that endures. The branches are your Paths, which take time to develop and can flex with the wind, and which feed the leaves, or your Goals. Clearly, the quality and quantity of your GRIT (roots) ultimately determines the strength of your Self (trunk), the height and health of your Paths (branches), and both the number and quality of the leaves, or the Goals you achieve. It takes impressive roots (GRIT) to grow a full canopy of Gritty Goals.

GRIT Gainer #1—GRITTY GOALS

One of the main reasons people, families, teams, organizations, and societies don't fulfill their potential and enjoy fulfilling results is because they don't set Gritty Goals. There are two simple steps: Set the GRIT Goal, then conduct a GRIT Check.

Note: The test of any tool is not its complexity, but its simplicity and its effect. How easy it would be to breeze through these questions and think, "Yeah, I kinda do this stuff now, but these are good thoughts. I suppose I should probably keep some of that stuff in mind." How easy would it be to underestimate the potential impact?

GRITTY GOALS

STEP ONE
Set the GRIT Goal with the GRIT Goal Question

Personal—*Given who and where I am, and all the resources and people I have with me or can reach out and get, what is the single most important goal I could possibly aspire to achieve?*

OR

Relational/Team/Organizational/Societal—*Given who and where we are, and all the resources and people we have with us or can reach out and get, what is the single most important goal we could possibly aspire to achieve?*

STEP TWO
GRIT Check

- Is it tough enough?
- How significantly and thoroughly will it test and tap our GRIT?
- Does it require a sufficient, if not a daunting level of sacrifice, struggle, even suffering in order to make it happen?
- Is it something few, if anyone, would even attempt, let alone successfully achieve?
- Does it represent the greatest possible, most powerful benefit(s)?
- Can you think of any goal that would be more "gritifying"— deeply gratifying due to A) how worthy the goal is, and B) what it potentially took to make it happen?
- If so, what would that grittier version be?

Whether you're a young kid with a dream like GottaHaveSole.org founder Nick Lowinger, or a seasoned game-changer like Elon Musk of Tesla and SpaceX fame, bettering the world all starts with a Gritty Goal.

So, grant yourself this favor. Pause and imagine for a moment if every serious goal you ever set A) was a GRIT Goal that B) passed the GRIT Check! Think how dramatically it could up your game, amplify both your Why and your Try, and forge your trail to a deeply "gritifying" career and life.

Think about work. Imagine if every serious goal your team and organization set was a GRIT Goal that passed the GRIT Check. What would that do to engagement, intensity, energy, momentum, and results? What would it do to competitive advantage, and the perception/loyalty of external stakeholders and customers, as well as the entire team who was signed up to make it happen?

Dare we think of our society? Imagine a president, prime minister, or premier who dared to ask these questions and take these steps to set Gritty Goals for their people, their world?

GRIT Gainer #2—GRITTY GAME PLAN

This tool has one simple purpose: to help you gritify your strategy or approach toward any goal. Take out the strategy or plan. Overlay, then ask these questions. It's pretty impossible to not arrive at a grittier Game Plan and result.

STEP ONE—Apply the GRIT Grid Cube

Smart

- Given who and where I am, and all the resources and people I have with me or can reach out and get, what is the single most important goal I could possibly aspire to achieve?
- How would the smartest/grittiest person/people I know approach this goal? What adjustments would they make to this plan to enhance its chances of success?

Good*

- How can I/we make sure the greatest number of people benefit from what we are doing, in the greatest possible way?
- What adjustments do we need to make to ensure the fewest number of people are harmed to the minimal possible degree?
- How can we do this even better, to bring the greatest possible happiness, comfort, and/or fulfillment to others?

Strong

- How can we demonstrate even greater overall GRIT?
- If we had only 10 percent more GRIT, where and how would we invest it to most dramatically increase our chances of success?

STEP TWO—Apply G-R-I-T

Growth—*What alternative angles, approaches, insights, and/or wisdom can we seek now to save us time and frustration later?*

- Whom could we talk to, or what resources could we seek to determine the smartest, best path to fulfilling this goal?
- What are the top two to three questions we would want answered to most strengthen our chances of success?
- Where could we go to get those answers now, instead of later?

Resilience—*What are the top two to three most potent challenges or obstacles we are likely to confront as we go forward?*

GRITTY GAME PLAN

STEP TWO *(continued)*

CORE Questions™

C Control. What are the facets of the situation we can potentially influence?

O Ownership. Where and how can we step up to make the most immediate, positive impact on the situation?

R Reach. What can we do now to minimize the potential downside of that adversity? To maximize the potential upside?

E Endurance. How will/can we get past it as quickly as possible?

Instinct—*Is this the best version of this goal? If we were to tweak it to make it even more compelling, clear, and worthy of our best, what would we change?*

- Is this the best approach, plan, path to get there?
- If we were to upgrade or update our path to at least increase our chances of getting there, what would we change?
- If our lives depended on our successfully achieving this goal as quickly and completely as possible, what adjustments/improvements would we make in our approach?

Tenacity—*Where would our next effort or attempt be best invested?*

- If we refused to give up, and kept at this for as long as it takes, what happens to our chances of success?
- How do we not sag, and make sure every attempt we make is our best?
- What can we do to amp up our next effort, so it's even stronger?

GRIT Challenge—GOOD*

Right this minute, while I'm writing this book, I received word that my 106-year-old grandmother, "Mum," passed away. True. I saw "Urgent Message," read it, and just found out. I had to step away to take a few breaths, stare out the window, shed a few tears. Then a big smile spread across my face, because I know with every fiber of my being, nothing would please Mum more than for me to talk to you about this subject.

You see, Good GRIT defined her life, her very essence. She simply refused to let sometimes massive, enduring, compounded struggles and suffering prevent her from being someone everyone considered amazing, and achieving a pretty optimal life. I won't burden or inspire you with her entire life story—including being the only female entrepreneur working on the gritty docks of Lake Erie, when she took over, grew, and sold a ship supply business in her mid-sixties. But suffice it to say, if Mum did one thing over all others, it was to demonstrate Good GRIT. It was her phenomenal capacity to be gracious, kind, loving, and magnanimous to pretty much everyone, pretty much all the time, in spite of whatever frustrations and struggles she had to endure to do so. She was an exemplar of Good GRIT, and that surely has a heck of a lot to do with why she felt she had such an amazing life.

Since writing the preceding paragraph, I attended and had the privilege of speaking at Mum's memorial service, which was packed with people who all said essentially the same thing, including this exact quote from the son of one of her dearest friends: "I've never known anyone like her, to be so accomplished and so kind. It's just humbling."

Having known and been infused by her goodness my entire life, I'd like to think the questions for "good" haunted her, as I hope they haunt you.

Thank you, Mum. Your Good GRIT made the world a better place.

"And whenever somebody says I can't do something, I always think, "How would I, if that were a possibility?"
— TIM DRAPER, SILICON VALLEY VENTURE CAPITALIST

GRIT Gainer #3—GRIT GANG

Secondhand GRIT

One way to grow GRIT is to form your GRIT Gang. You can do this by putting the flywheel effect into motion and intentionally leveraging Secondhand GRIT using a simple, two-step process. First, I will lay the foundation by briefly explaining Secondhand GRIT, why it matters, and how I believe it works at both a team and personal level. Then you will complete the two steps to form your GRIT Gang.

As you've no doubt witnessed in countless ways, so much of what does or does not get done in life is determined by the degree and manner in which people influence each other, for better or worse. We see this in action constantly with such essentials as integrity, hope, planning, choices, opinions, and, of course, aspiration. But this influencing principle is particularly potent when it comes to GRIT.

Pause for a moment to ponder the power of Secondhand GRIT. Did you ever consider how other people's GRIT might consciously or subconsciously affect yours? And vice versa? GRIT is not just something you overtly express through language; it is something you exude through action, manner, facial expression, breath, pace, gaze, posture, energy, stance, choice, sacrifice, struggle, emotion, mood, effort, and accomplishment. In a very real sense, GRIT permeates all facets of your being and expression. It also can permeate all facets of any given relationship.

Secondhand GRIT is real. And like secondhand smoke, at times it can be at least as potent coming from others as from you. GRIT is both overtly and covertly contagious. And you can use this power to grow yours and others'.

Secondhand GRIT—Team

You need not look far to spot the power of Secondhand GRIT at the team level. If you've ever been a part of any team digging deep to compete and/or striving to accomplish anything, you've likely felt the surge of determination, effort, energy, and resolve that can kick in, infusing the entire team, even in the darkest moments. Whether in victory or defeat, GRIT can determine not just the result, but also how everyone feels about the result.

GRIT Challenge—SECONDHAND GRIT IN THE NEWS

Valor if Not Victory: U.S.A. Shows Grit in Another Second-Round Exit

In the United States' loss to Belgium in the 2014 World Cup, their goalkeeper, Tim Howard, put on a historic performance with sixteen heart-stopping saves, and spurred the highest viewership of any U.S.A. World Cup match. It was a brilliant example of how one person's sheer relentlessness can elevate an entire team (and nation), enabling them to walk away from their overtime defeat with their heads held high, knowing beyond a doubt that they did their absolute best and gave it their all.

GRIT Challenge

I saw the opposite occur years ago, when I was advising a nonprofit organization. Their mission was essentially to preserve the pristine and fragile ecosystems in and near the Grand Canyon. This includes the Colorado River, the most important water source in the American West. Their efforts literally affect tens of millions of lives.

"John" (name changed) was the purpose-driven new executive director. A few short weeks into his tenure, a new challenge arose. A mining company was threatening to dump their toxic tailings into the Colorado River, which the staff biologists determined to be a genuine disaster in the making.

John immediately called a team meeting to attack this new threat. Apparently, there was a brief window of opportunity to voice opposition before the mining company put their machine in motion. They had three weeks to get ready. You could see the grim determination on everyone's face. Not knowing any better, John logically put his most knowledgeable expert in charge of preparing their case. Unknowingly, he also picked the person with the weakest GRIT.

Two factors pushed them into the GRIT pit. First, their expert felt the odds were so overwhelming, and the preparations so demanding, that he didn't do his job. Rather than digging deep, sacrificing some "me time," putting in the long hours, and galvanizing the resources to walk in prepared, he simply put together an anemic report, which read more like a resignation letter or eulogy than the kind of potent case they needed to upend their nemesis. It was pretty pathetic. This left the team walking into a knife fight blindfolded with one arm tied behind their back.

Second, when the moment of truth arrived, the organization's expert simply failed to speak up at the hearing, because ostensibly he felt it was already too little, too late. He concluded that the big, well-funded, corporate monster could not be slain, so why even try.

"We were completely screwed right outta the gates," he bemoaned, assuming his team would sympathize. "You could totally tell it was, like, already a done deal. You shoulda seen it. There they were, with all their high-priced lawyers and corporate types lined up. Hah! Classic. They even dressed casual, so they could get all cozy with the locals, as they seduced them with their promises of jobs, investment in community, blah, blah, blah. You should have heard the burst of applause when they showed the renderings for the new school they said they'd build. It was so depressing, and a total waste of our time to even be there."

What you really should have seen is the veins bulging in John's forehead as he held back his fury, and the tears in the team's eyes when they knew their battle was going to be quadruply difficult because their gritless teammate had let them down. Intellect without GRIT is not necessarily neutral. It can be a detriment. Fortunately, after years of gritty and scrappy effort, some seriously gritty leadership, and to the benefit of millions of people, the organization prevailed.

Both of these examples show the upside and downside of Secondhand GRIT at the team level. What about your one-on-one personal and professional relationships?

Secondhand GRIT—One on One

Secondhand GRIT works both ways, outbound and inbound. Think about the times when your GRIT, whether by word or deed, has inspired others to try harder, stick with some goal, give it another go, and see it through. You face such opportunities daily. Whether you see it or not, pretty much without fail, each time you dig deep, lean in, and give it your best, you inspire others to step up, rise up, and re-up.

> *"When you're more valuable, the people*
> *around you will do more to make it work."*
> **— SHERYL SANDBERG, COO OF FACEBOOK, AUTHOR OF *LEAN IN***

Flip the question: When *doesn't* your burst of authentic GRIT influence others? Secondhand GRIT is often invisible. How many people have you affected in this way over your lifetime? How many could (or should) have benefited had your GRIT been even greater? How many will be enriched as you put the power of Secondhand GRIT in motion?

Or perhaps you've been on the receiving end, enjoying the boost of hope, the redoubling of effort, and the shaking off of fatigue that comes when someone else—someone you trust and respect—ignites a fresh push. Maybe it was someone you viewed from afar, some story you heard about someone you've never met. Every year, when the grueling Tour de France race is aired, there is a surge in both frequency and duration of recreational bike rides (not to mention bicycle purchases) worldwide.

By viewing the best athletes digging deep to achieve their goals, millions of everyday riders try harder and longer, as a result. You can grow GRIT by experiencing and observing others demonstrate theirs. To make this less accidental and more deliberate, let's morph the Secondhand GRIT concept into a tool…

Step One—Do a GRIT Inventory

Rate your relationships. It's really pretty simple. It can also be profound. Do a quick inventory of all your current, key relationships. If you want to get the full value out of this activity, whip out a piece of paper or a tablet and list the actual names. Next to each, simply put either a G+, a G-, or a G.

Start with the G+. These are the people who fortify your GRIT, we hope in good, smart ways. When you think about the grittiest people you know or have known, especially the ones you really respect, how did or does their GRIT affect yours? Did they elevate your resolve? Do they raise your game and make you a better, stronger version of yourself? Who inspires your greatest GRIT? Whom can you count on to make you try harder, dig deeper, be more determined, and inspire you to struggle, sacrifice, even suffer to get what you want? These are your GRIT enhancers.

Next, consider and label any G's. These are the ones who are pretty GRIT neutral. They are neither a plus nor a minus. They aren't making any particularly gritty contributions, or necessarily bringing out the best in you or others. Is there any simple way, by giving them the right kind of challenge or engaging them with you in the right ways, that you can move them from a G to a G+?

Now add the G- next to those earning the honor. Think of the most grit-challenged, or gritless people you know. Who gives up, takes the easy road, backs down, or does anything they can to avoid struggle? Whom can you count on to fold, even sabotage his or her happiness, before ever fulfilling some big goal? How do these GRIT depleters affect you? Do they bolster or diminish your energy? Worse yet, do you find yourself squelching, even parking your GRIT to match, or at least to politely not outshine theirs?

Step Two—Form Your GRIT Gang(s)

You may wish to form separate GRIT Gangs for work and personal, then pull together the strongest of both into your A-level GRIT Gang. It's up to you.

As a leader or a manager, consider how important it is to define and deliberately assemble your GRIT Gang. The more potentially complex and frustrating it is, and the longer it takes to get things done, the more you desperately need your go-to GRIT Gang to make it happen. Here are three simple ways to help get the right people on your GRIT Gang, at work, so you achieve your most ambitious goals.

A) Measure their GRIT* with the GRIT Gauge™. It could be the smartest five minutes you ever required of them.

B) Ask them this question: "What is the single most difficult, frustrating, demanding, even excruciating long-term goal you ever tried to accomplish?" Have them tell you about it. How long it took. How they handled it. And how they'd feel about tackling more like that one.

C) Tell them you have some potentially impossible, but super-important goals that will require some serious sacrifice, and will be extremely demanding/difficult to achieve. Look for the light in the eyes. If they look away, lower their energy, and acquiesce, that's not good. If their spines straighten, their eyes light up, and they are visibly juiced by the opportunity, you're chances just got better.

Ideally, you'll do all of the above. And don't underestimate how profoundly they may feed off each other.

*Please contact us at info@gritgauge.com for more information on measuring your team's GRIT.

qualified. M. L. unless thorough. man Bldg. Barker. 1408 Chap.

MEN WANTED
for hazardous journey, small wages, bitter cold, long months of complete darkness, constant danger, safe return doubtful, honor and recognition in case of success.

Ernest Shackleton   4 Burlington st.

MEN—Neat-appearing pleasing personality, young men of and 40 to work between ages

Purported to be the original advertisement commissioned by Sir Ernest Shackleton to secure a crew for his legendary 1914 expedition to Antarctica aboard the *Endurance*. Legend has it that more than 10,000 men applied.

Secondhand GRIT is powerful. As you stare at the cold, hard truth, and embrace the powerful reality that grit begets grit, what adjustments do you need to make regarding whom you hang out with? With whom would you like to spend more or less time? Who on the G- list deserves your best energy, regardless? Whose GRIT do you intentionally want to feed?

If you could handpick the four to five people as your GRIT Gang—those who bring out your gritty best—who would they be? Imagine the effect something as simple as spending more time with your G+s and less time with your G-s might have. Many of the most powerful breakthroughs in human history were fueled by the synergistically elevated GRIT of a carefully selected group of individuals, who banded together to make the impossible possible.

In an important book, *Supersurvivors*, by David B. Feldman and Lee Daniel Kravetz, the authors highlight what the acknowledged thought leader on the subject, Dr. Richard Tedeschi, author of the *Handbook of Posttraumatic Growth*, has been saying for many years: Even in the most difficult circumstances, there are some people who end up better off as a result of what they've been through.

The research seems to indicate that at least as many people end up better off as end up worse off. Along with the best gritty experts—folks like Dr. Tedeschi; Dr. Mike Matthews at West Point; author Michael Kerrigan, founder of the Character Building Project; author and military psychologist Dr. Bret Moore; and Ken Falke, founder of both Shoulder 2 Shoulder, Inc. and the Boulder Crest Retreat for Military and Veteran Wellness—my team and I hope to considerably shift those odds, from PTSD to PTG.

The power of deliberately surrounding yourself and joining up with the right people toward the right goals cannot be overstated. There seems little doubt that deliberately forging and harnessing one's GRIT Gang can dramatically increase the chances of achieving gritty goals, in spite of—or perhaps with the assistance of—adversity.

The GRITified Life

Fifty years after standing on the terrace of Hearst Castle as an impoverished foreign college student scrapping and scraping to get by, KK and his wife, Haruka, stand a few miles down the coast, arm in arm on the veranda of their beloved Castello della Costa d'Oro watching the sun set over the Pacific Ocean. It's an apex moment.

KK's pocket is emptied of the cash he gave away to someone in need that day. But their hearts and souls are full with that deep sense of "gritification," the immense sense of fulfillment that only comes from having dug your deepest, sacrificed, struggled, and suffered for so long to make your dreams really come true.

Whatever your dreams, whatever gritty goal to which you dare aspire, you too can have your apex moment, your version of a gritified life.

Khosro Khaloghli with his wife, Haruka Minami Khaloghli.

Go with GRIT

This may be the final section of this book, but it is in no way your final chapter on GRIT. Assuming you've given the guts of this book a serious shot, and you close the cover having Grokked, Gauged, and Grown your GRIT more than ever before, then you can't help but do the most important thing, which is to gritify your life.

GRIT Happens! I started this book with a challenge: asking that you seek out those accomplishing anything worthwhile or impressive and determine what role GRIT played in their story. And in that way, you'd discover something simple but profound: GRIT *is* the story.

So it's only fair that I end with something simple but profound. The degree to which you optimize your GRIT—embark on the remaining hours of your life, showing your Smartest, "Goodest," Strongest G-R-I-T across all situations, in all contexts, and rising up to all rungs of the GRIT Ladder—is, very simply, the degree to which you optimize all facets and the entirety and purpose of your *life*.

ANNOTATIONS

Introduction—The Nitty-Gritty
Why GRIT?

p. 8   Ninety-eight percent of the 10,000 employers we surveyed demand it over anything else—including skills and qualifications—in the people they seek to hire, retain, invest in, and promote.
Independent study conducted in the United Kingdom and U.S., with sample spanning five continents, 2010–2014.

p. 9   According to Dr. Jennifer Green at University of Technology, in Sydney, grit is the overriding personal characteristic of high achievers with a disability.
http://www.smh.com.au/national/grit-the-key-to-job-success-20140710-3bq4f.html

p. 9   And as MacArthur Fellow Dr. Angela Duckworth has shown, grit even predicts who wins the National Spelling Bee.
http://www.ted.com/talks/angela_lee_duckworth_the_key_to_success_grit

p. 9   Grit is also predictive of both performance and retention among teachers, as well as which cadets at West Point's first-year "Beast Barracks" are more likely to stay, bail out, or stick it out.
https://upenn.app.box.com/s/81h02pjga2igfzsb0qk2
https://upenn.app.box.com/DuckworthPeterson

Your GRIT GPS—Mapping the Journey
Grow

p. 13   Based on real data and often-unsolicited feedback, these tools have enriched countless lives, relationships, families, careers, teams, and organizations, even societies.
www.peaklearning.com

Section One—The Basics
Grow

p. 33   James Ward is only nineteen years old and for the past five years has been homeless in Skid Row Los Angeles, moving between shelters, switching from school to school, and living in his mother's car.
http://www.huffingtonpost.com/2013/08/13/homeless-to-howard-james-ward_n_3749343.html

p. 43   I somehow doubt that Warner-Lambert Co. launched its revolutionary new diabetes drug, Rezulin, or Wyeth released Fen-Phen, to kill people.
http://listosaur.com/science-a-technology/10-former-wonder-drugs-gone-bad

p. 44   The world's charitable organizations save and enrich tens, if not hundreds of
        millions of lives each year.
        http://sciencelife.uchospitals.edu/2010/06/21/the-toll-of-good-intentions-gone-wrong

p. 50   Concordia University psychologist Carsten Wrosch investigates the nuances of
        giving up.
        *Wrosch, C., M. F. Scheier, C. S. Carver, and R. Schulz. "The Importance of Goal
        Disengagement in Adaptive Self-Regulation: When Giving Up Is Beneficial."
        Self and Identity, 2 (2003) 1–20.*

Section Two—Advanced
Grok

p. 101 There is growing evidence that the stress hormone cortisol, which elevates with a
        surge of stress, may actually decrease with chronic stress.
        http://www.scq.ubc.ca/stress-cortisol-and-the-immune-system-what-makes-us-get-sick

p. 104 These are the times you probably wished you had even more of the *right* kind of
        Emotional GRIT.
        *http://www.washingtonpost.com/blogs/wonkblog/wp/2014/03/27/divorce-is-
        actually-on-the-rise-and-its-the-baby-boomers-fault*

p. 105 Many teenagers prefer the simplicity of the virtual world over the
        "complexifications" of the real world.
        *http://www.theguardian.com/world/2013/oct/20/young-people-japan-stopped-
        having-sex*

p. 105 But among their three categories, "engaged," "not engaged," and "actively
        disengaged," 70 percent of employees live many of the prime hours of their lives
        on the dark side, being at least partially, if not actively disengaged, costing the
        U.S. economy roughly half a trillion dollars per year.
        *http://businessjournal.gallup.com/content/162953/tackle-employees-stagnating-
        engagement.aspx*

p. 107 On one hand—given that our tech tools in general are quite literally reshaping
        our brains and distracting us from minor responsibilities, like driving—clearly,
        the luxury of intense, protracted focus has all but dropped off the map.
        *http://www.psychologytoday.com/blog/the-power-prime/201212/how-technology-
        is-changing-the-way-children-think-and-focus*

        *http://www.huffingtonpost.com/2013/10/30/shocking-ways-internet-rewires-
        brain_n_4136942.html*

        *Small, Gary and Vorgan, Gigi, iBrain: Surviving the Technological Alteration
        of the Modern Mind (William Morrow Paperbacks, 2009).*

p. 125   During those same decades, education has become more stratified, with more well-off students graduating at higher rates, while middle- and lower-class students struggle to complete a degree.
Tough, Paul, "Who Gets to Graduate?" The New York Times Magazine, May 15, 2014.

p. 125   Not only is GRIT predictive of academic performance among disadvantaged and/or minority populations, it can also determine where you go in life.
Strayhorn, Terrell L., "What Role Does Grit Play in the Academic Success of Black Male Collegians at Predominantly White Institutions?" Journal of African American Studies, Published online: January 16, 2013.

p. 127   According to Dolly Singh, who worked for Musk for five years as the former head of talent acquisition for SpaceX, the moment their Falcon 1 rocket failed and propelled uncontrollably into outer space, Elon Musk showed what GRITty leadership is all about.
http://www.businessinsider.com/what-its-like-to-work-for-elon-musk-2014-6#ixzz3FacmKH7q

p. 133   To see if it were possible, I teamed up with national award-winning teacher Scott Swaaley on his pioneering GRITLab project at High Tech High School, a forward-thinking San Diego-based charter school focusing on project-based learning.
http://www.newsweek.com/2014/09/19/maker-movement-reinvents-education-268739.html

p. 136   In two separate analyses, Grohman found basic grit was not predictive of students' creative achievements and endeavors, including visual and performing arts, writing, scientific ingenuity, or even creative problem solving.
Sparks, Sarah D., "'Grit' May Not Spur Creative Success, Say Researchers," Education Week, published online, August 19, 2014.

Section Two—Advanced
Gauge

p. 142   You can then reassemble the pieces to get a holographic view of your current and potential GRIT.
Coyle, Daniel, The Talent Code: Greatness Isn't Born. It's Grown. Here's How (New York: Bantam Dell, a Division of Random House, Inc., 2009), 42.

Grow

p. 163   Valor if Not Victory: U.S.A. Shows Grit in Another Second-Round Exit
Longman, Jeré, "Valor if Not Victory: World Cup 2014: Against Belgium, U.S.A. Shows Grit in Another Second-Round Exit," The New York Times, July 1, 2014.

p. 168   Shackleton image courtesy of John Hyatt.

ACKNOWLEDGMENTS

I'm not sure it's genuinely possible to adequately express the gratitude I feel for everyone who in some way played a role in the inception, evolution, completion, and success of *GRIT*. But it's worth a shot.

To the millions of people across the globe who, through completing our assessments and programs, have contributed to the rigor and refinement of these teachings, my deepest thanks. Many of you have chosen to share our GRIT-based mindset and tools with countless others. I am immensely grateful.

I offer my humble thanks to my academic colleagues from around the world, including esteemed scholars Dr. Angela Duckworth at the University of Pennsylvania; Dr. Mike Matthews at the U.S. Military Academy, West Point; Dr. Sean R. Martin at Boston College; along with the burgeoning cadre of researchers worldwide exploring some facet of grit. Angela, thank you for your generosity and openness. You're an exemplar of the collaborative spirit.

Professors Scott Snook and Joshua Margolis, thank you for selecting and implementing my assessments and tools within the Harvard Business School MBA and Executive Education curricula for all these years. It has been an immense honor. You've made me—and all I do—better.

Laurie Stach, the visionary creator of the top-flight Launch Program at MIT, thank you for the privilege of using our assessments and teachings to screen and equip your select groups of young entrepreneurs with what it takes to turn their dreams into reality.

Sylvia Vogt and David James, thank you for the privilege of being part of your esteemed faculty for your Global Leaders Program at the Bosch Institute, at Carnegie Mellon. The best is yet to come.

To Dr. Jerilyn Grandy and Dr. Duanli Yan for your statistical brilliance. You give our independent studies their credibility, heft, and rigor. Jeri, you've always lived our message. Thank you for pioneering AQ and GRIT with us.

Jodi McPherson, thank you for having the vision and GRIT to bring GRIT into Pearson, so we can bring GRIT to the global world of education. It's long overdue.

Thank you Amy, Greg, Brian, Paul, Megan, Charlotte, Shannon, Travis, Steve, Dave, Robyn, Krissa, Christa, Kirk, Lizzie, Erin, Teresa, Robin, Lindsay, Erik, and everyone at Pearson for what we've done and what we are about to do. We will help transform education together.

Brian Tietje and Amy Baldwin, infusing GRIT into your about-to-be released, newest editions of *The College Experience* was so generous of you, as well as energizing and rewarding for me. We have great things to do together!

Scott Swaaley, thank you for letting us co-create the GRITLab at High Tech High and conduct some groundbreaking research together. You deserve every award and the many kudos you receive for being a trailblazer with GRIT. We have important work ahead.

Thank you, Michael Kerrigan of the Character Building Project, military psychologist Dr. Bret Moore, Ken Falke of Shoulder 2 Shoulder, Inc. and the Boulder Crest Retreat, and their extended teams. Together we will help countless military personnel and their families to achieve a grittier, healthier, and more fulfilling future.

Thanks to Dr. Sean Bryan, Chair, Department of Family Medicine, Greenville Health System, Greenville, South Carolina; Dr. Brent Egan, Department of Medicine, Division of General Medicine, Medical University of South Carolina; executive team member Tod Tappert, as well as Dr. Irfan Asif, who share the courage, vision, and GRIT to bring our principles to the adversity-rich world of health care.

Erik Weihenmayer, I thought climbing Everest blind showed GRIT, until I saw you one-man kayak the Grand Canyon. Your ability to suffer, sacrifice, struggle, and endure to achieve great things, not just for yourself, but also to benefit others, is unmatched. Thank you for the friendship and support.

No Barriers team, thank you for helping more and more people realize that "What's within you is stronger than what's in your way."

James Reed, my coauthor and dear friend, thank you for the tremendous work together, creating *Put Your Mindset to Work*.

Wolfgang Neumann, through your example, you teach your family, friends, and tens of thousands of employees at Carlson Rezidor what Good, Smart, Strong GRIT is all about.

Mike Crosby, the problem with your GRIT is you make it look so easy! Thank you for your decades of friendship, and for bringing the GRIT in INTEGRITY to life.

James Hart, your family, and team at SquareNerve, thank you for showing the GRIT to help build the guts of GRIT online.

Tom Schaff and Andy Miller, by bringing GRIT to small- to mid-sized companies, we are all learning and evolving GRIT together. Thank you for signing up for the Climb!

Michael Pimental, thank you for friendship and for bringing such honor to our work every time you facilitate a PEAK session. Your GRIT makes our GRIT better.

Gavin Dunn and my entire team at Phuel in Australia, thank you for all the years doing such an expert job bringing my teachings and tools to your continent. We've only just begun!

To PEAK's hundreds of precious clients: Thank you for being our laboratory, hiring us to bring our best to you and your people, to create an enduring impact on your enterprises and countless lives. This book would not exist without you.

To superstar literary agent Margret McBride: Thank you for bringing my work to so many, and for having the generosity of spirit to help me put *GRIT* on this new, promising path.

To my beloved and exceptional New York publicist, Jane Wesman, for sparking GRIT in the consciousness of countless people through her mastery.

To my brutha, Phil Styrlund, and his coauthor of *Relevance,* Tom Hayes: Thank you for your generous insights, resources, guidance, and support.

To Mark Pitzele at Thomson Reuters for shepherding our project with world-class expertise and finesse.

Elizabeth Baniaga, your illustrated animations brought some of our examples to life.

To Julie Sullivan and her team, including Mary Ross: How can we ever thank you for the decades of dedication and expert design work? Everything we put in our clients' hands is both praised by them and appreciated by me.

To the entire PEAK Team: Your Why and your Try are constantly tens. I'm humbled by your heartfelt dedication to the cause, bringing GRIT to countless enterprises, schools, institutions, and lives. How can I ever thank you?

Shannon Roberts, you deserve special thanks and mention for throwing your all into this book.

Tina Miller, in many ways this is as much your book as mine. How can I ever thank you enough for being its project manager and parent?

Dr. Jeff Thompson, twenty-one years as my "partner in Climb" at PEAK! If that's not GRIT, I don't know what is. Thank you for the decades of friendship, memories, and life-changing work.

To my mother, Sandra Stoltz: So much of what you taught me informs this book. A good chunk of this is definitely your fault!

To my family: You do me the highest honor of all by not only clearing the way for me to dedicate myself guilt-free to the task at hand, but also by living what we teach, each of you striving to become exemplars of Optimal GRIT, and now infusing that in your children. You inspire me to be better, and grittier, every day.

Sabina, your example of doing all you can to not let anything get in the way of doing your best continues to inspire.

Mum, you were the matriarch of *GRIT*. Thank you for showing us how it can be done.

To my wife, Ronda: I could have saved thousands of hours and hundreds of pages by simply printing a single photo on the cover … your face. You are my most stellar exemplar of Optimal GRIT. Your ability to endure, actually harness chronic challenges with such grace, beauty, and strength elevates anyone fortunate enough to know you. Nothing I write can do justice to what you exude or to the depth of my love for you.

And to *you,* my reader, for picking up and delving into *GRIT:* May it fuel your success in all that you pursue, and may it help you forge a truly "GRITifying" life.